THE DHAMMAPADA

THE DHAMMAPADA

With an introduction to the life and times of Lord Buddha and his philosophy

Kadambari Kaul

INDIALOG PUBLICATIONS PVT. LTD.

Published in February 2007

Reg. Office
Indialog Publications Pvt. Ltd.
O - 22, Lajpat Nagar II
New Delhi - 110024

Telefax: 91-11-29830504/29835221
www.indialog.co.in

Development Centre:
B-58, Sector-VI
Noida (UP)
Telefax: 0120-4238791, 4349990

10 9 8 7 6 5 4 3 2

Printed at Brijbasi Art Press Limited.

ISBN 81-8443-006-X

CONTENTS

To all the upholders of truth who are no more.

In memory of my great grandfather Late Sir Tej Bahadur Sapru and my grandfather Late Justice P.N. Sapru.

ACKNOWLEDGEMENT

Writing the "Dhammapada" has indeed been a very long and self-fulfilling journey. For Buddhism is a subject that is very close to my heart, and through this book, I have had the opportunity to express some of the profound "truths" uttered by Siddhartha Gautama the Buddha, 2,500 years ago, as he preached his doctrine along the central areas of the Ganges Basin.

A big "thank you!" to the entire team at Indialog Publications – my publisher, Mr. Basant Pandey, Mr. Gagan Das, the marketing manager who has very efficiently co-ordinated various activities throughout, Mrs. Keerti Ramachandra, my commissioning editor, and last but not the least, to my very discerning and meticulous editor, Dr. Anjana Srivastava. Thanks Anjana for everything!

A special thanks to Mrs. Maina Bhagat, Consultant, Oxford Bookstore, Kolkata, for her help and support throughout this project.

I also wish to thank my parents, Jitendra Narain and Malti Sapru, my husband, Kapil, and my daughter, Gayatri, for encouraging me to embark upon this project and for their patience in listening to the verses and other excerpts from my manuscript, as I progressed along with it.

Once again, thank you everyone for helping me turn my dream into a reality.

Kadambari Kaul

DHAMMAPADA – AN INTRODUCTION

INDIA IN THE SIXTH CENTURY B.C.

This, then, is the philosophy of the Buddha. This is all there is, in this slim book of verse called the "Dhammapada", that is needed to guide us along the path to salvation.

For "Dhamma" means truth, law or righteousness and "Pada" means path, and the Dhammapada is the path of righteousness laid out by the Buddha, assuring all those who choose to follow it, deliverance from evil. It is the holy path that leads them towards the deathless shores of Nirvana.

The Dhammapada is perhaps the most popular book of the Pali canon, a part of the Tipitakas or the three baskets of the Buddha's philosophy, namely the Sutta Pitaka, the Vinaya Pitaka and the Abhidhamma Pitaka, containing the discourses of the Buddha, his discipline and Buddhist metaphysics respectively. It is, in fact, an important part of the canonical literature of the Khuddaka Nikaya or the fifth section of the Sutta Pitaka.

The verses of the Dhammapada are the poetic utterances of the Buddha that have been collected from various sources of the Pali canon. As regards the date of the composition of the Dhammapada, it can be traced to the history of the Tipitakas or the Pali canon that was settled by the monks who held a council at Rajagriha, shortly after the death of the Buddha. In fact, it was at the first council, that the monks memorized the teachings of Lord Buddha, according to the formulae they devised regarding the authenticity of his doctrine.

The doctrine of the Buddha was thus handed down orally by the monks for almost three to four centuries after his death. It was only in the first century B.C., during the reign and under the orders of King Vattagamani of Ceylon, that the canon was written down by the Buddhist priests who, on observing the perdition of the people, wanted to preserve the religion of their land. Thus, it was sometime in the first century B.C. that the earliest Buddhist scriptures, the Tipitakas, were written.

In fact, in the Mahavamsa no mention is made of the existence of any Buddhist scriptures, even during the reign of the Mauryan Emperor Ashoka in the third century B.C. According to the Mahavamsa, Mahinda, Ashoka's son who was sent to Ceylon to spread Buddhism, rehearsed the Tipitakas under the tutelage of the monks who imparted the canon orally to him. It was under his influence that the King of Ceylon, Devanampiya Tissa, as well as the people of the country, converted to Buddhism.

The view that the Tipitikas or the Buddhist canonical literature was first written in the first century B.C. is further supported by the works of the Buddhist scholar Buddhaghosa, the author of the commentary on the Dhammapada. Buddhaghosa who travelled from Magadha to Ceylon in the fifth century A.D. drew most of his information from the Pali canonical literature written in the first century B.C. This was according to him, by and large, the same as that settled by the monks at the first Buddhist council held at Rajagriha.

However, the Sutta Pitaka or the basket of the Buddha's discourses with which we are presently concerned, since the Dhammapada falls into this category, is divided into five nikayas or collections of works. The Khuddaka Nikaya or the fifth section of the Sutta Pitaka of which the Dhammapada is a part, contains the largest number of treatises of the Pali canon. Although the meaning of Khuddaka is "small" or "minor", it contains the two major Pitakas, namely the

Vinaya Pitaka and the Abhidhamma Pitaka and also brief doctrinal notes in verses, the birth stories or Jatakas, as well as the history of all the Buddhas.

The Dhammapada, perhaps the most important book of the Khuddaka Nikaya since it contains the philosophy of the Buddha in a nutshell, is divided into 26 chapters and consists of a total of 423 verses. There is a certain timelessness in the poetry of the Dhammapada, as one finds embedded in the verses, the philosophy of the Buddha, which governed by the universal values of self-liberation and compassion, transcending all barriers of religion, class or creed, never fails to touch the hearts of those who hear it.

The Buddha out of his boundless compassion, using poetry and parables, spoke to the people in their language and thereby succeeded in carrying a message aimed at the salvation of humankind to the world at large. His teachings were centered round the universal subject of human suffering and the path that led to the cessation of suffering.

It is noteworthy, that the Buddha was born amidst the rise of Indian civilization, into an urbanizing world, that was exposed to a new set of socio-cultural values that were at variance with the ones held previously. The Varna or class system that stratified Indian society into the Brahmin, Kshatriya, Vaishya and Sudra classes since the dawn of the Aryan civilization in the second millennium B.C., was suited to the old warrior society and found it hard to accomodate the new occupations that came into existence with the rise of cities. According to the old Varna system, the elite that comprised the Brahmins or the priestly class and the Kshatriyas or the class of kings and warriors ruled over the Vaishyas who were husbandmen and the Sudras or serfs. The Sudras who were at the bottom of the social scale were condemned to a life of servitude to the three upper classes.

However, the introduction of money, an increase in trade and commerce, accompanied by the emergence of a wealthy and influential merchant class, created a new elite that did not quite fit into the old social order. The simple rural way of life was gradually giving way to more complex forms of urban life. The rather insular society of the Indians had become cosmopolitan and sophisticated.

The Indians found themselves quite at sea in their new social world as they struggled to find a universal law or moral code to govern their behaviour. It was therefore only natural that the era witnessed an intellectual movement of philosophers and renouncers who questioned the prevalent values and beliefs of the people, forming their own theories on religion and life, in an attempt to resolve the socio-cultural conflicts of the time, enabling the suffering multitudes to come to terms with reality. The Buddha belonged to this class of people who had walked away into homelessness, propounding doctrines aimed at alleviating the suffering of mankind.

To make matters worse, the Brahmanic religion of the people that was a sort of animism, in which the forces of nature were worshipped as Gods, was also a sacrificial cult that demanded the performance of elaborate animal sacrifices and rituals in order to appease these Gods. The Brahmins had turned these sacrifices into expensive affairs in an attempt to extort money from the people. There also existed amongst the Indians at this time, much belief in tapas or self-mortification as a means to salvation, magic and superstition, and a growing tendency towards monism, the belief in the supreme soul from which all creation emanated.

Moreover, knowledge of the Vedic scriptures was confined to members of the priestly class, and an elite group of Kshatriyas who because of their privileged birth lived in a state of enlightenment while the rest of the people remained in ignorance. It was in this age of questioning and despair, that Siddhartha Gautama, the founder of a new unorthodox cult that was later referred to as Buddhism, was born in the sixth century B.C. He gave hope to the people, by challenging the supremacy of the Brahmins, as he showed them the path that led to the realization of the ultimate truth.

LIFE OF GAUTAMA BUDDHA

The centres of change and civilization at the time of Gautama Buddha's birth in the sixth century B.C., lay to the south of the republic of Kapilavasthu that was governed by his father

Suddhodhana. These included the central areas of the Ganges Basin as well as the areas that lay to the north of it. They were inhabited by a number of warlike tribes amongst other people.

There existed at that time, alongside kingdoms of considerable importance in these areas, several republics, some of which were democratic in their style of functioning while others tended to be more aristocratic. A number of tribal chiefs had succeeded in establishing kingdoms and in the Buddha's time the struggle for supremacy lay between the southern kingdoms of Kosala and Magadha.

However, the Buddha, who was named Siddhartha, was born in the sixth century B.C., in the Lumbini Garden, near Kapilavasthu, Nepal. He belonged to the Gautama clan of Sakyas who claimed their descent from the sun. Siddhartha Gautama was not in the strict sense of the term, the son of a king, but the son of the tribal chief of the Sakya republic of Kapilavasthu who had assumed the title of raja. He was, nevertheless, an aristocrat as the Gautama family belonged to a class of wealthy landowners.

His father Suddhodhana whose name meant "pure rice", was democratic in the manner in which he conducted the affairs of the state. Perhaps the democratic principles on which the Buddha later founded the Sangha were inherited from his Sakyan forebears. The Sakyas were a proud tribe of warriors of Aryan descent who lived at the foothills of the Nepalese Himalayas, along the northern edge of the Ganges Basin.

Thus, into this illustrious family of Sakyan rulers was born the liberator Gautama Buddha. His father named him Siddhartha, which means "he who has accomplished his goal." Shortly after the birth of Siddhartha, it was predicted by the great sages at the court, that he would either become a chakravartin, a universal monarch, or he would renounce the world, ultimately becoming a Buddha, an enlightened being.

Pained by the prophecies of the astrologers and weakened by the strain of childbirth, Queen Maya the mother of Siddhartha died shortly after his naming ceremony. After a year of mourning had passed, Suddhodhana married Mahamaya's sister Mahapajapati Gautami and entrusted Siddhartha to her care.

Suddhodhana who had never quite forgotten the prophecy of an astrologer at court, that his son on seeing an old man, a diseased man, a corpse and an ascetic would renounce the world and become a Buddha, wasted no time in isolating his son from the harsh realities of the world that lay beyond the palace walls.

He created a secluded world for Siddhartha, where the young prince was surrounded by all things bright and beautiful, encouraging him to indulge in every form of sensual pleasure. Despite all the luxuries of a princely life, Siddhartha found life in the palace "cramped and cabinned." Being spiritually inclined, Siddhartha, was more absorbed in thoughts concerning the deeper meaning of life rather than the pursuit of sensual pleasures. On observing the serious disposition of his son, Suddhodhana decided to get him married, hoping that the duties of a householder would prevent him from renouncing his princely life. At sixteen, Siddhartha was married to his cousin Yashodhara, a Koliyan princess, and a niece of his mother Maya.

After thirteen years of marriage, a son was born to Siddhartha and Yashodhara, whom they named Rahula, meaning "fetter" or "tie." Despite the birth of his son, life in the palace did not hold any charm for him. He was filled with a longing to step out into the world that lay beyond the palace walls.

Suddhodhana, on sensing his son's desire to step into the world outside, ordered a jewel-fronted chariot with four of his finest white Sindhi steeds to be kept ready to take his son on his first journey into the streets of Kapilavasthu. He commanded his men to beautify the streets of Kapilavasthu, in order to hide all the ugly and painful sights of human suffering from him. However, the gods willed it otherwise.

As the handsome young prince drove into the city accompanied by his charioteer Channa, he saw an old man, his body bent and worn out with age, walking along. The sight revealed to him the impermanence of beauty and youth. On his second journey into the streets outside, he beheld a diseased man, a skeletal figure walking on the road. Then, on his third journey into the outside world, he saw a corpse being carried by a group of mourners and realized the inevitability of death. On his fourth journey into the streets of Kapilavasthu, Siddhartha saw an ascetic with a begging bowl, wandering about without a care in the world despite all the vicissitudes of life. It made him realize that all forms of human pain and suffering were the outcome of desire and attachment to an impermanent world.

These four visions proved to be a turning point in Siddhartha's life. Realizing the transient nature of his family and princely existence, he resolved to detach himself from them. It dawned on him that even attachment to one's loved ones could be a source of suffering. Suffering could only be overcome by renouncing this world of pleasure and pain, by seeking that which was permanent, the state of eternal bliss that was Nirvana.

Thus, in the spring of his twenty-ninth year, while his wife and son were asleep, Siddhartha stole quietly out of the palace grounds on his horse Kanthaka, accompanied by his charioteer Channa, in search of the ultimate truth. This event is known as the Great Renunciation, as it marked the end of his existence as Prince Siddhartha of Kapilavasthu.

After leaving the palace, Siddhartha silently rode towards the river Anoma in a forest close to the Himalayas. There, he cut off his long tresses, the symbol of a Kshatriya, removed his ornaments and royal robes and handed them over to Channa along with his horse Kanthaka with strict instructions to return to the palace. He then donned the simple garb of an ascetic, the colour of earth, and with a begging bowl in hand, walked southwards towards Magadha, the kingdom of Bimbiśara from where he proceeded to the hermitages of the most renowned sages of that time, Alara Kalama and Udakka Ramaputta.

Under them, he practised yogic meditation, which progressively led to higher states of consciousness. However, it did not lead to the cessation of suffering. Gautama realized that while yogic meditation did indeed lead to tranquil states of mind for long periods, these states were actually temporary as they were caused and conditioned by the meditator's technical skills. They did not lead to the realization of the ultimate truth.

So, in his quest for the ultimate truth, Siddhartha then experimented with self-mortification as practised by some of the most renowned sages of that time. He joined the company of five bhikkus who practised a severe form of penance in the jungles of Uruvela. There he immersed himself in meditative thought and almost starved himself to death. Had it not been for the timely offering of a meal of milk and rice by a girl named Sujata, Siddhartha would have been dead. After he ate the meal, his thoughts cleared and he soon regained his strength. He then realized the importance of the middle path that lay between extreme asceticism and self-indulgence in providing the mind and body with all the nourishment they needed while practising advanced forms of meditation. It was also at this time that he became convinced about the inefficacy of the systems of yoga and self-mortification in the attainment of the ultimate truth.

Siddhartha was now convinced that the truth lay within oneself, and could only be realized through a process of introspective meditation or vipassana. Thus, he evolved vipassana or insight meditation from the yogic meditations that he had learnt from his teachers Alara Kalama and Udakka Ramaputta. Vipassana was a mindful and energetic form of meditation in which the meditator, by analyzing the minutest aspects of his physical and mental states, acquired a moral and intellectual perfection that eventually led to the realization of the ultimate reality.

So, from Uruvela, Siddhartha who had now lost faith in all forms of external aids such as animal sacrifice, prayers, yogic meditation and even self-mortification in the attainment of salvation, walked on tirelessly till he reached Bodhgaya in modern Bihar where he sat under the shade of a pipal or bodhi tree and practised vipassana. Finally, at the age of thirty five while meditating under the bodhi tree, on a full moon night, Siddhartha Gautama attained Buddhahood or enlightenment, as the ultimate truth was revealed to him.

Prince Siddhartha who had now become Gautama, the Buddha, out of compassion for humankind, then left Bodhgaya, spreading his doctrine wherever he went. He travelled far and wide along the central areas of the Ganges Basin, and spent time spreading the Four Noble Truths that were revealed to him at the time of enlightenment at all the great cities of Sarnath, Kasi, Magadha, Kosala, Kosambi and Campa. The Buddha travelled northwards as well, to the lands occupied by the Vajji confederacy, Mallas, the Kalamans, the Sakyas and Koliyas.

Shortly after his enlightenment, he founded the Sangha or the order of Buddhist monks at Sarnath where he first preached his doctrine to the five bhikkus in whose company he had practised the severe austerities at Uruvela. Later, Yasa the son of a wealthy merchant and his family, Ananthapindika another wealthy merchant of Savatthi and several other merchants joined the Sangha. Apart from the city merchants, the renowned sage Kassapa, the chief of the Jatilas or Uruvela Brahmans and several other Jatilas also became his disciples. They were amongst the most prominent members of the Sangha. Buddha's parents, wife, and son Rahula also converted to his faith.

The Buddha who spent the last days of his life preaching the truth along the dusty plains of North India finally died of mortal causes at the ripe old age of eighty in Kusinagar in modern Bihar. It was the last meal of wild boar's meat that he had taken, cooked by Chunda the metal-worker at Pava that caused his sickness and death. When he died amidst a crowd of mourners, it was with the happy feeling of having shown people the Path of Righteousness that would lead them towards the blissful state of Nirvana. Indeed, Gautama Buddha remains one of the greatest thinkers from the east whose philosophy even 2,500 years after his death continues to have a profound impact on human civilization.

PHILOSOPHY OF THE BUDDHA

The Buddha who was well versed in the Brahmanic scriptures founded his doctrine on the philosophy of the Upanishads. He rejected the sacrificial literature of the Vedas but imbibed from the philosophy of the Upanishads that stressed on realizing the ultimate reality that was Brahman, the Atman or the Universal Soul through rapt contemplation and detachment from all earthly ties.

However, unlike the Upanishads, the ultimate reality, in the Buddha's philosophy was not the Atman or Brahman, but the "Dhamma", the eternal truth that could only be realized through the practice of morality and meditation. The Buddha regarded the realization of the ultimate reality as Nirvana or enlightenment whereas the Upanishads regarded the realization of the ultimate reality as the union of the human soul or self with the Universal Soul or Brahman.

The Brahmanic religion of the Indians in the sixth century B.C. had over the years been made increasingly ritualistic by the priests. Elaborate animal sacrifices and rituals performed by the Brahmins or priests, at all major events in an individual's life such as "annaprasan" or the feeding of grain ceremony, or "upanyana", the thread or initiation ceremony of the three upper classes, had become expensive affairs.

Moreover, the language of the Vedas had changed so drastically that it was now understood by only a small elite school of Brahmins who guarded their knowledge jealously in order to retain their power over the religious lives of the people. It was believed that to displease a Brahmin who through his spiritual knowledge had access to the Almighty, was to incur the wrath of the Gods who could wreak havoc on the offenders. Endowed with mystical powers, the Brahmins were more feared than respected by the Kshatriyas and the rest of the populace.

Although the Buddha revered a number of Brahmins for their wisdom and learning, he challenged their supremacy in matters of religion and learning and their supreme position in the structure of Indian society. A liberal and a democrat at heart, he propounded a doctrine that was comprehensible to the elite and laity alike, which at a stroke broke the barriers of the class system by throwing open the doors of immortality to humankind. His relatively simple doctrine showed people the way of realizing the ultimate truth by believing in the Four Noble Truths and following the Eightfold Path of Righteousness that gradually expiated all their sins. The path negated the influence of the Brahmins who till then had acted as intermediaries between the individuals and the ultimate reality.

According to the Buddha, anyone could in his lifetime without any external aid in the form of prayers, animal sacrifice or yogic meditation, through strenuous effort, by believing in the Four Noble Truths and steadfastly treading the Eightfold Path of Righteousness, attain enlightenment or Nirvana and thus be released from the odious cycle of rebirth.

It was a revolutionary thought as it challenged the religious beliefs of the Indians and the supremacy of the Brahmins, by making people rely on themselves in the attainment of Nirvana. A pragmatist, the Buddha never spoke of God or the Creator but the Law of Righteousness that governed the universe. It was in his description of the ultimate reality or Nirvana, the state of eternal bliss or enlightenment, that transcended all joy and sorrow, heaven and hell, that he differed with the Upanishads that regarded the ultimate reality as Brahman or the Universal Soul.

His entire philosophy, was built on the foundation of the Four Noble Truths, which though apparently simple were pregnant with meaning. The First Noble Truth as preached by the Buddha was the Existence of Suffering. The Buddha stressed upon the all-pervasive nature of suffering that was an inescapable part of human life.

In his philosophy, suffering on a larger scale encompassed birth, death, pain, decay, disease, sorrow, separation and lamentation. On a smaller scale, suffering included the minor frustrations experienced by an individual in his daily life such as a job undone, a wish unfulfilled, or a missed opportunity. He said, "Union with the unpleasant is suffering, separation from what is pleasant is suffering, not achieving what one desires is suffering."

Since everything in this world was imperfect, impermanent and ever-changing, the Buddha preached that some of the most joyful states of existence in the life of an individual, whether physical or spiritual, had within themselves the germ of suffering, as they were never the same for two consecutive moments. Indeed, as experienced by most of us, all happy and pleasurable states of existence are sooner or later replaced by anxious and unsatisfactory states of existence.

He further preached that the combination of five aggregates or groups that constituted an individual, the "self" or "I", namely matter, feelings, perceptions, thoughts and lastly consciousness, were always in a state of flux, imperfect and ever-changing, and therefore also included in the term "suffering."

According to the Second Noble Truth or the Arising of Suffering, as stated by the Buddha, thirst (tanha) or the craving for knowledge or existence was as much a cause of suffering as the thirst for sensual pleasures, material wealth, or power. As indeed according to the Buddhist monk Walpola Sri Rahula and as found in the ancient Buddhist scriptures - "It is thirst which produces re-existence and re-becoming, bound with passionate greed, which finds fresh delight now here, now there, namely, thirst for sensual pleasures, thirst for existence and becoming and thirst for non-existence (self-annihilation)."

The Buddha preached that "tanha" or thirst was the immediate and most palpable cause of suffering that led to the pain of continual rebirth in this cycle of continuity, Samsara. He explained to his followers that this thirst was caused by ignorance about the true nature of reality and the delusion that all worldly pleasures were everlasting. In his philosophy, everything in this world, right from the changing of seasons, world affairs, down to the conception of the smallest idea in the minds of men, was impermanent and ever-changing, governed by the Law of Karma or the law of cause and effect.

Even the "self", the "I" to which we are so attached, and for whose preservation and glorification we work so hard, was governed by the Law of Karma, and was a product of a series of causes and effects, that could be traced back to the dawn of consciousness of the individual. The self was in reality, a combination of physical and mental energies that were always in a state of flux, and held together by the thirst for existence that led to the pain and suffering of continual birth and death. It must be borne in mind, that the desire for existence and becoming, is a powerful force which accompanied by the dying thoughts of an individual, lives on after death, taking the form of a new life according to the karma, the deeds and misdeeds of the previous life.

The Buddha therefore impressed upon his followers that it was only through the extinction of all selfish desires, particularly the desire for existence and continuity, and the dispelling of ignorance through ethical conduct and insight meditation that suffering could be overcome and Nirvana attained.

The Third Noble Truth or the Cessation of Suffering as revealed by the Buddha states that Nirvana, the realization of the Absolute Truth, can be attained upon the extinction of thirst and all defilements and most importantly the destruction of the false idea of "self." He further preached that the "truth" was within ourselves and could be discovered by treading the Eightfold Path of Righteousness or the Fourth Noble Truth. Thus, the Eightfold Path as shown by the Buddha consists of:

1. Right Understanding – Correct understanding of the Four Noble Truths.
2. Right Thoughts – Thoughts of kindness, love and compassion.
3. Right Speech – Abstaining from all evils of speech.
4. Right Action – Upright behaviour that promotes peace and harmony in society.
5. Right Mode of Livelihood – An honourable way of earning one's living.
6. Right Effort – The energetic will to cultivate only a positive state of mind.
7. Right Mindfulness – Awareness of one's immediate physical and mental states.
8. Right Concentration – That which leads the mind to a state of equanimity, bordering on Nirvana.

Thus, according to the Buddha's philosophy, the veil of ignorance that hung between the individual and the ultimate reality, once removed by extinguishing all forms of selfish desires and attachments, treading the Eightfold Path of Righteousness, in accordance with the Dhamma, the moral law, eventually led to salvation. Moreover, following the Eightfold Path did not depend on the priesthood but on human effort, in the practice of morality and meditation which led to the attainment of enlightenment. Nowhere in the Four Noble Truths did the idea of a God or the Universal Soul creep in. The Buddha stressed on the importance of ethical behaviour and meditation, as he entreated people to work out their own salvation with diligence. He advised his disciples not to accept any doctrine out of blind faith, tradition, respect for authority or hearsay but to accept it on the basis of their faith in the efficacy of the doctrine, born out of conviction through their own personal experience.

Although the Buddha acknowledged the efficacy of yogic meditation that he had learnt from his teachers Alara Kalama and Udakka Ramaputta in improving one's power of concentration, which he felt was essential in the attainment of salvation, he realized its limitations as it did not lead to the cessation of suffering. The Buddha believed that while yogic meditation progressively led to more refined levels of consciousness, it provided the meditator with only a temporary relief from his earthly sufferings, as it depended on his technical skills at manipulating causes and conditions within himself. Since these heightened states of consciousness attained through yogic meditation were "caused and conditioned", they were in the Buddha's opinion only "tranquil abidings in the here and now."

Convinced that the truth lay within oneself, the Buddha preached that it was only through the practice of introspective meditation, leading to a dramatic transformation in the emotional and mental make-up of an individual while steadfastly treading the Path of Righteousness, that salvation could be attained. Since, in his philosophy, the ideas of self-liberation and compassion were inextricably linked, he enjoined his disciples to meditatively cultivate compassion towards all sentient creation as a habit of mind.

Thus, he evolved vipassana or insight meditation from the yogic meditation that he had learnt from his teachers Alara Kalama and Udakka Ramaputta. Vipassana was a wakeful and energetic form of introspective meditation, whereby the meditator by constantly and dispassionately analyzing the minutest aspects of his immediate physical and mental states, acquired a moral and intellectual perfection, that gave him a penetrating insight into the Dhamma, the moral law, enabling him to transcend this caused and conditioned world as he entered the blissful, uncaused and unconditioned state of Nirvana.

Nirvana or enlightenment in the Buddha's philosophy was the ultimate reality that was unborn, uncreated, and unoriginated. It was opposed to Samsara or this world of experience and change that was born, created, and originated. It was a state of eternal bliss and enlightenment, the realization of the oneness of the ultimate reality that lay beneath this world of duality and separateness. Nirvana was the Absolute Truth that was unanalyzable, unageing, and deathless, attained when the fires of lust, hatred and ignorance were extinguished in the mind. It marked the cessation of suffering as it released the individual from the painful cycle of rebirth.

However, it must be borne in mind that although the Buddha upheld the lofty ideal of renunciation in order to attain Nirvana, he did not view man in isolation but as a member of society. His philosophy was suited not only to the monks who had chosen the renunciant way of life but also to the rather imperfect standards of morality of the laity who had to live in this world and perform their household duties.

Thus, the moral code he evolved provided people with guidelines on moral conduct and ethical behaviour based on the universal values of self-liberation and compassion that enabled them to co-exist in a complex, urban society. Indeed, compassion for humankind was the chief motivating factor in the Buddha preaching his doctrine to the multitudes who were groping in the dark for a universal law to guide their actions.

Compassion, however, in his philosophy was analyzed in its simplest form as sympathy for others. On a slightly higher scale, compassion meant rejoicing in the well-being of others and at its highest level, compassion meant treating all human beings with loving-kindness despite their failings. In fact, it was the Buddha's sentiment of loving-kindness which devoid of any cultural, racial or religious prejudice, pervaded the entire universe and made him treat saints and sinners alike. This appealed to the people, who happily became followers of the Buddhist faith. It was simply unthinkable for the compassionate Buddha to condemn even those who had strayed from the Path of Truth and taken to evil ways. The Buddha believed that it was ignorance that was misleading them in their quest for everlasting peace and happiness.

Indeed, one of the main reasons for Buddhism's striking success in his lifetime and later in becoming a world religion was that it was essentially a religion of universal love and compassion that upheld the principles of equality and righteous living, as it showed people the path to peace, prosperity and ultimately enlightenment in this world itself. Furthermore, Buddhism's relatively easy adaptability to other faiths even while it clung tenaciously to its own beliefs, as well as the Buddha's discretion in segregating politics from his philosophy, also contributed in ample measure to its acceptance in cultures quite alien from the culture of the land of its origin.

It must be borne in mind that the Buddha in all his discourses addressed the universal problem of human suffering, showing people the way to cope with the trials and tribulations of earthly existence. His doctrine dealt primarily with the subject of human suffering, the cause of suffering and the cessation of suffering.

A keen observer of world affairs, the Buddha exercised great discretion in matters of state and governance, although evidence from the way he conducted the affairs of the Sangha points to the fact that he was a democrat who preferred the republican form of government. Yet, the Buddha succeeded in receiving patronage from the most powerful kings of that time, King Pasenadi of Kosala and King Bimbisara of Magadha, who in due course converted to his faith. Although he never really approved of the inequalities of the caste system, he never condemned it but simply propounded a doctrine that transcended all barriers of class, caste and creed, as it showed people the path to a happier state of existence and ultimately, to salvation.

Perhaps the most unique contribution of the Buddha to religious thought was his revolutionary theory of "Anatta", "no-self" or "no-soul" that rejected the Brahmanic theory of Atman upheld by some of the most renowned sages of that time. He challenged the Brahmanic belief of the atman, the human soul or self as being a part of the immortal Universal Soul or God, and denied its existence as an independent entity, distinct from the mind, that transmigrated from one birth to another. He preached that the soul and the mind were one and the same thing.

In fact, when his teachers Alara Kalama and Udakka Ramaputta both upholders of the theory of Atman tried to impress upon him that the soul was the "I", the "self", the doer of all deeds and the thinker of all thoughts, he viewed their belief to be rooted in error and a manifestation of their ego and vanity. The Buddha preached that belief in the "I", the "self" or "ego" created selfhood, which in turn gave birth to feelings of egotism, envy and hatred. Salvation could only be attained by the destruction of the illusion of self.

Thus, the Buddha propounded the theory of "Anatta" or "no-self" which denied the existence of an independent and immortal soul or self. He stated unequivocally that there was in reality no self within or outside an individual, in the universe or anywhere outside of it. Instead, he laid stress on an individual's thoughts and deeds or their karma that endured the cycle of rebirth and spoke of the transmigration of character rather than the transmigration of soul.

The Buddha who was inclined towards agnosticism based his observations and theories on "provable truth", on all that he "had experienced and seen for himself" during deep insight meditation. This led him to liken one's belief in the Universal Soul or God to a man who proclaims he is in love with the most beautiful woman on earth and is unable to name her or describe her form, and dismissed it as illusory.

He did not dwell on the subjects of Creator and the origin of creation as he realized the limitations of human thought in explaining the deep mysteries that surround them. Moreover, he felt that discussion of these subjects would only end in vain speculation, and divert the minds of his followers from more important matters relating to the practice of morality and meditation, which were essential in the attainment of salvation. The Buddha was a pragmatist who simply dealt with the universal subjects of pleasure and pain, common to all individuals, as they existed in the "here and now" rather than concerning himself with the past or the future.

In his philosophy, God or the Creator was replaced by the timeless Law of Righteousness that governed the universe and lives of men in this world and beyond. Those who abided by the law by treading the Noble Eightfold Path of Truth were assured of salvation. It was not a negative view, as by showing people the Noble Eightfold Path, he had in fact opened the doors of immortality.

A product of his times and the milieu into which he was born, the Buddha as mentioned earlier, borrowed several ideas from the Upanishads upon which he built his theory of transmigration. A firm believer in the Law of Karma, the law of cause and effect, the Buddha preached that it was only man's karma or deeds that endured the cycle of rebirths, and that man was heir to his karma. Nothing in this universe, neither natural phenomena nor human events, was without a cause or effect. In fact, even an individual's thoughts that fashioned this world were caused by certain preceding conditions.

He further preached that an individual's present birth was the outcome of his karmas of all his previous births, right from the dawn of his consciousness, and that his karma in this birth would have a bearing on his next life. It was only one's karma that determined one's destiny in this world and beyond. Good karma, in accordance with the Dhamma, led to a better rebirth while bad karma led to rebirth in a lower grade of existence. The Buddha, who on attaining enlightenment had gained an insight into his unconscious, could recall his past existences, through the various stages of his evolution from a tree and even earlier, to the time he attained Nirvana and became Siddhartha Gautama, the Buddha.

He believed in the power of the mind, comprising thoughts and experiences that influenced an individual's actions. The Buddha preached that all impulses, actions, and reactions were the outcome of the choice of good and evil thoughts present in the mind. He regarded choice or the intention, the mental action that preceded an individual's thoughts and actions as his karma and therefore preached the cultivation of a positive state of mind. Hence, it was the choice that was of ultimate significance in the Buddha's philosophy, for having so chosen, a person acted through his thoughts, speech, and body, the consequences of which he had to bear in this life and after. He believed that good thoughts untainted by desire, greed or attachment to worldly things, led to happiness in this life and after, eventually emancipating him from the cycle of rebirth. Thus, the world in his philosophy was fashioned by an individual's choices.

It was on account of an individual's karma or deeds of previous births that he was born into this world of suffering where he was subjected to old age, pain, disease, separation, and death. The Buddha preached that in this birth itself, through belief and the practice of the Four Noble Truths, one could deliver oneself from evil and attain Nirvana.

The Buddha who had in his lifetime attained Nirvana, laid down the moral law that has ever since influenced human thought. What is remarkable is that his philosophy that was propounded 2,500 years ago in Bodhgaya, in modern Bihar, India, has found acceptance right through the ages, down to this present age of globalization, amongst scientists, theists, agnostics, atheists and humanists who take his name with reverence the world over.

Thus, in the poetry of the Dhammapada, Siddhartha Gautama, the Buddha, guides us through a conflicting maze of thoughts, in an ever-changing, imperfect world, towards the kingdom of righteousness where he dwells evermore in a state of absolute bliss.

DHAMMAPADA

THE PAIRS

It is our thoughts that make our mind
Our characters and our world
We are what we think
Speak ye and act with an evil mind
Suffering follows you
Everywhere
In this world and beyond
Just as the wheels of the cart
Follow the oxen that draw it.

It is our thoughts that make our mind
Our characters and our world
We are what we think
Speak ye and act with a pure mind
Happiness follows you
Everywhere
In this world and beyond
Like a shadow that never leaves.

"He hurt me, he cheated me, he abused me, and he defeated me."
The minds of those where such thoughts dwell

Like a furnace
Red and hot
Burning with the fires of hell
Remain in bondage to error and hatred.

"He hurt me, he robbed me, he abused me, and he defeated me."
The minds of those where such thoughts have ceased to dwell
Like the tranquil waters
Of a heavenly lake
Clear and blue
Shall be freed from error and hatred.

Hatred can never overcome hatred
Neither great wars nor revenge
It is only love
Pure and sublime
That can overcome hatred.

This is the law
Ancient and eternal
And those who know that their lives must end
Learn to live in peace and harmony.

Just as the wind blows away a weak tree
Mara breaks through the minds of the weak
Of those who are indolent and gluttonous
Uprooting their thoughts
With the promise of worldly pleasures
And their thoughts full of desire
Cannot see the truth
They are asleep and unmindful
And know not that sorrow will soon befall them.

Just as the wind cannot blow away a mountain
Mara cannot break through the minds of the strong

And uproot their thoughts
With the promise of worldly pleasures
For their thoughts are free from desire
They are awake and disciplined
Abiding by the law
And know that sorrow now cannot befall them.

He is not worthy of the yellow robe
For he is without self-control
And untrue
As he recites the verses
With an impure mind
And a heart full of desire
He then is not a monk.

He is worthy of the yellow robe
For he is self-controlled
And true
As he recites the verses
With a mind that is pure
And a heart untainted by desire
He then is a monk.

Those who see falsehood in truth
And truth in falsehood
Their judgement full of error
Cannot know the truth in all its glory
For they are deluded.

Those who see falsehood as falsehood
And truth as truth
Their judgment free of error
Know the truth in all its glory
As they follow right desires.

Just as an ill-thatched house that allows the rain to enter
Like a weak fortress
With numberless apertures and unguarded
So also, an unreflecting, untrained mind
Allows passion to make its way
And lead it on the path of evil

Just as a well-thatched house does not allow rain to enter
Like a strong fortress
Without apertures and well guarded
So also, a reflecting, trained mind
Does not allow passion to make its way
And lead it on the path of evil.

The evil-doer suffers in this world and beyond
He suffers always
Pained by the evil of his misdeeds.

The righteous man rejoices in this world and beyond
He continues to rejoice
In the goodness of his deeds.

The evil-doer who cares not for the law
Suffers in this world and the next
And continues to suffer
Pained by the evil of his misdeeds
And more suffering awaits him
As he enters the abode of evil.

The righteous man who abides by the law
Rejoices in this world and the next
And continues to rejoice
In the goodness of his deeds
And more joy awaits him
As he enters the abode of the good.

It is not the number of scriptures you read
Nor the holy words you speak
But your thoughts and deeds
And the eternal law
That decide your destiny.

And if you do recite holy verses
Not practising what you preach
You are then no better
Than the shepherd
Counting another man's sheep.

And so,
You shall not partake
Of the joys of a spiritual life
And attain the highest wisdom.

It is better then
To recite a few verses
With a heart clean and pure
Practising what one preaches
Abiding by the Dhamma
The moral law
Ancient and eternal.

For then you shall partake
Of the joys of a spiritual life
As you attain
The highest wisdom.

So give up folly, hatred, and greed
Desire and passion
Tread the Path of Truth
Sharing the way
And you too shall be delivered.

EARNESTNESS

Those who are earnest
And ever-mindful
Of their thoughts and deeds
As they walk upon the Path of Truth
Shall taste the fruit of their earnestness
That is immortality
The ineffable bliss of Nirvana
As they enter the kingdom of righteousness.

And the thoughtless
Unmindful of their thoughts and deeds
Are as good as dead
They shall live on
In this world of sorrow
Decay and death
And continue to suffer
As the gates of the kingdom of righteousness shut before them.

And life eternal is the reward
For those who strive earnestly
And mindfully
Along the path of the awakened
And they shall one day

Cross the river of death
Whence there is no return.

While the thoughtless
Who strive not
Shall be reborn
In this ocean of birth and death
That is Samsara.

The wise understand this
And rejoicing in the tranquillity of meditation
Have found the greatest joy in wisdom
And freedom
From earthly sufferings
Born out of strenuous effort
Following earnestly
The path of the awakened
And meditating mindfully
Upon the Four Noble Truths.

And meditating earnestly
Ever-mindful of their thoughts and deeds
Have the wise ones
Attained the highest bliss
Of life eternal
That is Nirvana.

And glory is his
Who arouses himself
And is always earnest
Self-restrained and compassionate
Reflecting on his thoughts and deeds
Feelings and perceptions
Abiding by the law
Learns to live in peace and harmony.

So awake
Before it is too late
And reflect earnestly
Upon your thoughts, feelings and perceptions
Abide by the Dhamma
And you shall see
The golden light of truth
Grow within you.

The wise man
Living in this world of experience and change
That is Samsara
May thus create for himself
Through earnest meditation and self-control
An island of peace and tranquillity
That is Nirvana
In a sea full of troubles
That no flood can overwhelm.

And fools
Unmindful of their ways
Give in to sloth
Seeking sensual pleasures
In the "here and now"
Come to grief
But the wise
Guard their earnestness
Their greatest treasure.

They seek not sensual pleasures
In the "here and now"
But meditate earnestly upon the Dhamma
Seeking that which is permanent
The eternal bliss of Nirvana
And delight in the realization of the truth.

So guard ye against lust and sensual pleasures
Of the "here and now"
And sloth
As you break away
From all the fetters of earthly existence
For they bring only sorrow
In this life and after
Be mindful and meditate earnestly
And ye shall discover true happiness
In this life and after.

From the tower of wisdom
Reached through moral conduct
And earnest meditation
The wise man
From his abode of truth
Blissfully
Looks down upon the sorrowful crowd
Like the man standing on the mountain top
Gazes at the dwellers
On the dusty plains below.

Earnest amongst the slothful
The wise man advances
Like a race horse on a field
Swiftly
Mindful amongst those asleep
Leaving them all behind
As he reaches his ultimate goal.

It was through earnest effort
That Indra
Rose to lordship
Of the Gods
Of the Vedic pantheon.

Earnestness is the way of life
To be praised
And thoughtlessness the way to death
To continual existence in this world
Of pain and misery
To be derided.

Rejoicing in his earnestness
A mendicant
Fearing the perils of thoughtlessness
Like an evil to be shunned
Burns the bonds
Of earthly existence
Through the spiritual fire
That burns within him.

The mendicant
Rejoicing in earnest mediation
Continues treading
The Noble Eightfold Path
There is no falling back for him
For he is close
To the habitation of the truth
Nirvana.

THE MIND

Like a fletcher whittles
And aims his arrows
So also a wise man mindfully
Meditating upon his thoughts,
Unstable and fickle
Feelings and perception
Of the world outside
Directs the stream of his thoughts
Rushing forth aimlessly
Towards its ultimate destination
Enlightenment.

The thoughts of a man meditating
Rooted in desire, envy and hatred
Move about restlessly
Without direction
In anguish
Desperately trying to escape
The evil hand of Mara
Like a fish out of water
Its natural habitat
Lying breathless,
And struggling for life
Quivering on the sandy shore.

Health and happiness belong to those
Who control their thoughts
Mindfully
Meditating upon
The Four Noble Truths
Directing their thoughts
Along the Path of Truth
Against the tide of falsehood
Towards the ultimate reality
That is Nirvana.

The greatest happiness lies
In the stillness of one's thoughts
Subtle and ever so elusive
Mastering
And liberating them
From the fetters of worldly existence
And treading steadfastly
The lonely Path of Righteousness.

Through concentration
And a single-mindedness of purpose
The meditator directs his thoughts
That wander at will
Along the Path of Truth
As he embarks upon an inward journey
Away from the distractions of the world outside
Liberating himself
From the evil bonds of Mara
And attains the highest freedom
Nirvana.

The meditator
Reflecting upon his thoughts and deeds
Feelings and perceptions

And his bodily states
Is truly wise
He masters his thoughts
As he purges his mind
Of all defilements
And lives on
In the tranquillity of Nirvana.

The troubled mind
Blinded by worries and cares
Of earthly existence
Can never understand the Dhamma
The eternal law
Stumbles along
The path of falsehood
Groping in the dark for a way
To end its pain
For it cannot see the ultimate truth.

The tranquil mind
Untroubled by worries and cares
Of earthly existence
Understands the Dhamma
Ceases to think
And consider
What is right or wrong
Transcending both good and evil
It is beyond judgement
For it has realized
The ultimate truth.

Alas! This body
That we preserve so well
Is like a fragile jar
Which shall dissolve one day

But your thoughts will live on
So make a castle of your mind
And protect it always
From evil and transgressions
Making it the abode of truth
As you conquer Mara
And his forces of destruction
With the weapon of your wisdom.

And remember always
This body shall lie discarded and despised
Lifeless upon the ground
Like a burnt piece of faggot
Useless and forgotten.

So beware! Be ever-mindful
Guard your thoughts
Your greatest treasure
From envy, hatred and greed
For thoughts unguarded
Can do more harm
Than one's worst enemies.

And remember
No one
Neither your parents nor your friends
Can do you good
The way your thoughts
Well trained and guarded
Cleansed of all evil
Can as they liberate you
From the pain of continual birth
And earthly existence.

FLOWERS

Just as the garland maker
Chooses with care
The most beautiful and rarest of flowers
So must you
With care
Choose the well taught Path of Truth
And walk steadfastly
Towards the kingdom of righteousness
For then you shall go
Beyond the realms of sorrow and death
This world and the world of Gods
And attain Nirvana.

And remember
The disciple who chooses
The well taught Path of Truth
Laid out by the Buddha
Shall go beyond the realms of sorrow and death
This world and the world of Gods
And attain the highest freedom and bliss
Nirvana.

Knowing then
That this body

Like a mirage
A frothy wave
In a bottomless ocean
Shall dissolve one day
Into nothingness
Break through then
Mara's flower tipped arrows of temptation
And attain life eternal
That is Nirvana.

Like a flood
That sweeps away
A sleepy village
Death overtakes
The unmindful and unrighteous
Before their desires are fulfilled
For they spend their lives
Not in quietude and contemplation
But in earnest pursuit
Of worldly pleasures
Gathering life's flowers.

The wise
Absorb all that is beautiful and pure
From nature
And cause it no harm
Like the bee
That takes care
Not to mar
The beauty of the flower
From which it draws
Its sweet nectar.

Sit not on judgement
On the words and deeds
Of those around

But sit back
And contemplate
Upon thine own words and deeds.

Empty are the words
And meaningless
Of those who do not practise what they preach
Like a beautiful flower
Bright and colourful
Without fragrance.

Meaningful are the words
Beautiful and pure
Spoken from the depths of truth
By those who practise
What they preach
Like a beautiful flower
Bright and colourful
Full of the fragrance
Of truthfulness.

So let this life then be
A garland of good deeds
Like a garland
Made of many lovely flowers.

The fragrance of truth
Of the enlightened one
Is stronger than
The fragrance of sandalwood and the tagara flower
The lotus and jasmine
That cannot travel against the wind
But the fragrance of the enlightened one
Travels far and wide
Against the strongest wind.

How much stronger
And more beautiful
Than the fragrance of the jasmine
Lotus or the tagara flower
Is the fragrance of virtue
Of the enlightened one!

The fragrance of genuine goodness
Is so much finer
Than the fragrance of sandalwood and the tagara flower
Lotus or the jasmine
It pervades the entire universe
As it rises to the world of Gods.

And so, the enlightened one
Ever-mindful and earnest
Whose fragrance of goodness
Fills every quarter of this universe
Is freed by his wisdom
From the bondage of Mara
And he dwells
In eternal peace and tranquillity
Nirvana.

And like the lotus
That grows out of the depths of slime
Bright and beautiful
Towards the sun
Filling the air with its delicate fragrance
So also the good deeds
Of the true follower of the Buddha
Fill the universe
With their sweet fragrance
As he shines with the intensity of truth
Amongst blind mortals
Bringing hope and joy to those around.

THE FOOL

Long is the journey
For the weary
And long is this cycle of continuity
Of birth and death
That is Samsara
For those who know not
The Dhamma
The eternal law
Like the night
Endless and long
For those who lie awake
Troubled by worldly cares.

And if you find no one
To walk with you
The lonely Path of Truth
It is better then to walk alone
Than to seek the company
Of the foolish
Who delude themselves
With thoughts of their possessions
Of their wealth and sons
The truth is
That nothing is theirs

For even they
Do not belong to themselves.

The fool
Knowing that he is foolish
Has some wisdom
For he has embarked upon
The journey to salvation
To the attainment of the supreme wisdom.

But the fool
Thinking that he is wise
Is indeed a fool
And he continues to suffer
In this ocean of birth and death
As he tastes the bitter fruit
Of his foolishness
He cannot escape
The effects of his karma
Of his past or present.

Just like the spoon can never know the taste of soup
So also the fool can never understand
The Dhamma
The eternal law
That governs this universe
Even while he spends
An entire lifetime
In the company
Of the wise.

Just as the tongue knows the taste of the soup
The wise man perceives the Dhamma
The eternal law
Even while he spends

A moment in a day
With the enlightened.

The greatest enemies of the foolish ones
Are themselves
For having done deeds
Rooted in falsehood
They bring remorse
And suffering to themselves
In this world and beyond.

So bear in mind always
That those deeds are selfish
Which when done
Bring pain and sorrow to the doer
But good deeds when done
Rooted in the truth
Bring lasting peace and happiness
To the doer
In this world and beyond.

Pleasurable and sweet
Are selfish deeds
Bringing momentary joy
To the doer
But alas!
When those selfish deeds
Begin to ripen
He tastes the bitter fruits
Of his selfishness.

Prayers, rituals and self-mortification
Fasting and eating from the blade of kusa grass
Can never deliver the fool
From his evil

And he is indeed not worth a sixteenth part
Of those who understand the Dhamma
The eternal law.

Like fresh milk
That takes time to curdle
A selfish deed
Also takes time
To bring pain and sorrow
To the doer
Burning him slowly
With the fire of evil
Like the fire
That smoulders under the ashes.

Not caring to know
Or understand
The Dhamma
The eternal truth
The fools misuse their knowledge
As they writhe in agony
Pained by the evil of their misdeeds.

The fools craving for power and prestige
Even in monasteries
Desire precedence
Amongst monks
And praise from all
Deluding themselves
That they are right
And others wrong
As their pride and passions grow
Causing rebirth
In this cycle of continuity.

Be careful then
In choosing the Path of Truth
To eternal deliverance from evil
And remember
That the path of profit and pleasure
Is in reality
The path to death and destruction.

So strive along
Oh! Disciples of the Buddha!
The Path of Righteousness
Enduring all the pleasures and pains
Of worldly existence
With forbearance
Till you attain the supreme wisdom
And shine from afar
Like untarnished gold
With the intensity of your goodness.

THE WISE MAN

Unattractive is the path
Full of hardship
Trod by the wise man
And if he shows you this path
Follow him
And you shall reach
Your destination
Where there shall be unearthed
Hidden treasures
That will lead you towards the kingdom of righteousness
Nirvana.

Harsh are the words
And unkind
Spoken by the wise man
But these words
Spoken from the depths of truth
Tell you what you really are
So let him admonish and chasten you
As he guides you along the Path of Truth
Towards the island of eternal bliss
That is Nirvana.

And so the wise man
Is loved evermore
And deeply
By the good
But not the bad
As he spreads
For the welfare of all
Nothing but the truth.

Be careful then
And seek not
The company of fools
And those who are not good
But seek instead
The company of the wise
The noble and true
Who illumine your mind
With words of wisdom
As you walk along
The Path of Righteousness
Towards salvation.

Purify your hearts
As you contemplate
And abide by the Dhamma
The moral law
Revealed by the wise man
And then rejoice
In the goodness of your deeds
And the serenity of your mind.

Just as engineers
Direct the flow of rivers
Archers straighten their arrows
And carpenters carve wood

So also the wise man
Skilled in meditation
Mindfully cultivating
Wholesome frames of mind
Shapes his thoughts
As he purges them
Of error, egotism and desire.

Like a rock
Solid and strong
Remains unshaken
By the endless gusts of strong winds
A wise man
Remains unshaken
And impervious
To both praise and criticism
As he lives on
Protected by the goodness of his deeds.

And like the still, clear waters
Of a heavenly lake
Their minds become tranquil and pure
When they hear the Dhamma
The eternal law.

Undeterred
By happenings around him
The wise man walks along
The Path of Truth
His thoughts untainted
By the world around
His utterances
Are never vain and hollow.

And so he walks on
Untouched by fortune and misfortune
And he desires nothing
Neither wealth nor power
Not even children
Or success through unfair means
He is free from all worldly desires
Virtuous and wise
He is truly noble.

Few are those
Who cross the river of death
And reach the deathless shores
Of Nirvana
For most
Run back and forth
Along the shores of earthly existence.

But the wise who abide by the Dhamma
The eternal law
That governs this universe
Well taught to them
Shall one day be delivered from evil
And they shall go beyond the river of sorrow and death
To the island of eternal bliss
That is Nirvana.

Leaving behind the darkness of ignorance
The wise ones follow the infinite light of truth
Renouncing everything
Their homes and loved ones
And all the pleasures of worldly existence
As they purify their thoughts
And live in joy and freedom
Walking along the path to salvation.

And their thoughts rooted in the seven elements of enlightenment
Of mindfulness and meditation
Wisdom, energy and joy
Serenity and equanimity
Are purged of all sensual desires and attachments
As they dwell in absolute bliss
Freed from this cycle of continuity
Of birth and death
Rejoicing in their freedom
They enter the gates of immortality
That is Nirvana
Becoming lights unto themselves.

THE ARHAT

The Arhat or saint
Is he who has gone beyond suffering
Who has reached the end of his journey
As he liberates himself
Through the nobility
Of his thoughts, words and deeds
From the fetters of worldly existence
And lives in eternal bliss and freedom
That is Nirvana
Uncaused and unconditioned.

Homeless
Without possessions
He strives ceaselessly
Along the lonely Path of Truth
Like swans
Leaving all that is theirs
As they fly away
From their home
The lake.

And just as hard it is
To trace the path of flight
Of birds in the sky

So also hard it is
To trace the footsteps
Of the selfless
Without possessions
Living on alms in a world of freedom
Who through temperance in food
And control of senses
Know the true meaning
Of bliss and unconditioned freedom
Nirvana.

He who has renounced his pride
And subdued his senses
Controlling them like a skilled charioteer
Who trains his horses
The Arhat
Is envied by the Gods
Dwelling in the highest heavens above.

And patient like good earth
The Arhat
Stands firmly like a threshold
To life eternal
And pure like a lake
Clear and blue
Without mud
He shimmers in the morning sunshine
Liberating himself
From the painful cycle of birth and death.

Having renounced this world of name and form
And all selfish desires
He has attained Nirvana
The eternal truth
That language cannot describe

For Nirvana is the uncreated, unborn, unoriginated
Found in the depths of meditation
When the mind is stilled and passions no more
When every thought, word and deed of his is calm
And the illusion of self destroyed
Freeing him now who is an Arhat
From this endless cycle of birth and death.

The Arhat is the noblest of us all
His thoughts, words and deeds
Free from thirst and attachment
Arising from the unfathomable depths of truth
Carry him towards the island
Of eternal peace and tranquillity
Amidst this ocean of birth and death
That is Samsara.

And wherever he goes
In the village or forest
Land or the sea
With his wisdom and senses well controlled
He brings joy to those around
And comfort to aching hearts
As the genuine goodness of his deeds
Pervades the world around.

Severing all worldly ties
He seeks not the fulfillment of sensual pleasures
And desiring nothing
He finds happiness
Even in the solitude of forests.

THE THOUSANDS

Better than a speech
Of a thousand words
Hollow and meaningless
Senseless and without feeling
Is one word of the Dhamma
The truth
That extinguishes the fires of passion, hatred and greed
And brings with it
Peace and joy
To the troubled mind.

Better than a poem of a thousand verses
Or a hundred poems of senseless verses
Vain and without depth
Is one word of the Dhamma
The truth
That quietens the mind
Leading it on the Path of Righteousness
Towards enlightenment.

The greatest conqueror of all
Is he who has conquered the self
Who has vanquished the forces of evil
Within himself
And entered the hallowed portals of Nirvana.

The conqueror then basks in the glory
Of the conquest of the self
A conquest more glorious
Than another's
Who has conquered a thousand times
A thousand men on the battlefield
So bear in mind always
That victory over oneself
Is immeasurably greater than the victory over others
Which even the mightiest Gods
Cannot turn into defeat.

Better than performing a thousand rituals
For a hundred years
Or tending the sacrificial fire
For a thousand years
Is a moment in one's lifetime
Spent paying homage to the wise
For he is the truth
Who illumines our minds
With words of wisdom
As he leads us
On our journey towards salvation.

Vain are gifts and offerings
And sacrifices made for a year
To forces unknown
That we can neither see nor comprehend
They are not worth a quarter
Of the homage
Paid to the wise
Even for a moment
As we follow them on the Path of Truth.

So remember always
Homage paid to the wise
Bring the four gifts of
Health, happiness, beauty and long life.

Better than a hundred years
Spent in pursuit of sensual pleasures and mischief
With an evil and unreflecting mind
Is a day spent in wisdom and virtue
In contemplation
Of our thoughts, words and deeds
Treading steadfastly the Path of Truth.

Better than a hundred years
Spent in ignorance or delusion
Unrestrained and undisciplined
Enslaved to the self
Working in vain
Towards its continual existence
In this world of change and experience
Is a day
Spent in quiet reflection
Of the Four Noble Truths
Believing in them and practising them
As we walk upon
The path to enlightenment.

Better than a hundred years
Of weak and idle living
Is a day
Spent in hardship and strength
Striving for the truth
The eternal bliss of Nirvana.

Better than a hundred conditioned years
Spent in ignorance
And bondage to error
Is to live a day
In wisdom and freedom
Contemplating
All things caused and conditioned
That arise and pass away
Into this ocean of birth and death
As we perceive
The true meaning of life.

And indeed better than a hundred years
Spent in ignorance
Is to live a day in solitude
Reflecting upon
The Four Noble Truths
And perceiving the unageing, deathless and formless state
Of Nirvana
That awaits all those
Who tread steadfastly
The Path of Truth.

Better than a hundred years
Spent in ignorance
Not perceiving the Dhamma
The eternal law
Is a day spent
Meditating upon the Four Noble Truths
And perceiving the Dhamma
That liberates us
As we abide by it
From selfish desire
And the pain and suffering
Of worldly existence.

EVIL

Hastily
With a mind undistracted
By worldly pleasures
A man should walk upon
The Path of Truth
And never should he be
Slow or slack
In doing deeds that are good
And refraining from those that are bad
For his mind
Veering from the Noble Path
Shall then begin to rejoice in evil.

Let a man not commit a sin
That cleaves to him
Through many births
For painful is the result
Of the accumulation of evil deeds
Which when repeated
Become a habit
That endure
The endless cycle of birth and death.

Let a man continue to do
Deeds that are good

Again and again
Making it a habit
For the good he does
Lives after him
Bringing him peace and happiness
In this world and beyond.

An evil deed once done
Fulfills our sensual desires
Bringing pleasure to the doer
But alas!
Sorrow soon follows
When the evil deed begins to ripen
And bears the bitter fruit of unrighteous behaviour.

A good man
Enjoys no peace or happiness
Even while doing
Deeds that are good
Rooted in the truth
But when his deeds begin to ripen
He tastes the fruits of his goodness
In the tranquillity of his thoughts.

Let no man be deluded
As he walks upon the path of evil and pleasure
His thoughts full of selfish desires
That evil shall not come near him
For as a pot
Is filled slowly to the brim
With tiny drops of water
So also a man
Slowly becomes
Full of evil.

Be hopeful then
And think not
That goodness shall never come near thee
For as a pot
That fills slowly to the brim
With tiny drops of water
So also a wise man
Slowly becomes
Full of goodness.

Just as a wealthy merchant or traveller
Shuns the highwayman
Standing on the dangerous road
Or a man in love with life
Avoids poison
So also should a wise man
Avoid the path of evil.

Just as poison has no power
Of bringing harm
To an unwounded arm
So also evil cannot befall
The righteous
For they are protected
By the goodness of their deeds.

Evil shall befall those
Who wrong the innocent
Recoiling on them
Like fine dust
Thrown against the wind
Falls back upon the thrower.

The horrors of hell
Await those who have sinned

While the good go to heaven
And others are reborn
In this world again
But the righteous
The awakened ones
Enter the gates of immortality
Nirvana
That transcends joy and sorrow
Heaven and hell
As they dwell evermore
In this blissful, unageing, deathless state.

There is no place
In the entire universe
Neither in the sky nor on land
Neither in the mountains nor on the high seas
Where a man can escape
The consequences
Of his evil deeds.

Suffering and death
Is the fate
Of the evil-doer
And there is no place
In the entire universe
Neither in the sky nor on land
Neither in the mountains nor on the high seas
Where he can escape
The pain of death and continual existence
In this bottomless ocean
Of birth and death
Samsara.

PUNISHMENT

Punishment and death
Are the bitter fruits
Of evil deeds
Done in ignorance of reality
So bear in mind
That everyone lives in fear
Of punishment and death
Loving life as you do
So do unto others
As you would have them do unto you
And do not kill or cause to kill.

The pain and suffering
Of worldly existence
In this ocean of birth and death
Shall follow you
If you seek happiness
In causing pain and injury to others
Who seek happiness just as you do
But if you seek happiness
In doing noble deeds
That bring happiness to others
You shall be happy in this life and after.

Speak softly
And gently
Words of wisdom
That calm the minds of others
That they may
Speak kindly to you
For harsh words
Unkind and malicious
Causing pain and suffering to others
Shall rebound on you.

So bear in mind
If your mind
Is still like a broken gong
And you abstain from all evils of speech
You shall find happiness
In this life and after.

With his staff in hand
The shepherd
Drives his cows to newer pastures
In the same way
Old age and death
Carry you forward
To re-existence
In this cycle of continuity
And the selfish
Who cannot comprehend the truth
Continue to do evil deeds that consume them
Like a burning fire.

They are guilty
Who harm the innocent
And they shall suffer
For their misdeeds

Of this life and previous lives as well
And they shall reap
What they have sown
In this life and after.

Suffering will come to them
In ten different ways
And they may suffer grief, infirmity and serious illness
Legal prosecution, insanity or a fearful accusation
Family bereavement or loss of fortune
The burning down of their house
Or meet with a serious accident
And upon death
They shall be devoured
By the fires of hell.

No amount of penance
Fasting, matted hair or sitting motionless
Can deliver a man from evil
If his thoughts are impure
But one whose mind is tranquil and chaste
Full of noble thoughts
Controlled and disciplined
Who leads a peaceful life
Even if he wears fine clothes
Shall be delivered
For he is a true monk
A Brahmin.

Just as a well trained horse
Galloping swiftly
On the path to victory
Needs no whip
So also a well trained mind
Disciplined whilst treading the Path of Truth

Needs no prodding
From the world
To follow the Dhamma
The eternal law.

So emulate the well trained horse
Abide by the Dhamma
Have faith and meditate mindfully
And you shall attain
The supreme wisdom
As you go beyond sorrow
And dwell in eternal bliss and freedom
Nirvana.

Skillful like the irrigator
Who channels water to parched fields
Like the archer who straightens his arrows
Or the carpenter who carves wood
Is the wise man
Who perceives reality
Correctly
And fashions his thoughts
His life and his world
In accordance with
The Dhamma.

OLD AGE

The world is afire
Burning with the passions of envy, hatred and greed
Why then do the ignorant make merry?
Shrouded in darkness
Laughing their way along
The path of evil and pleasure
Instead of seeking
The Path of Righteousness
And the eternal light of truth.

This body of ours
Is merely an illusion
A painted image
Beautiful and fragile
Enlivened by our ever-changing stream of thoughts
And it harbours within itself
Like all things created
The germs of disease, decay and dissolution.

There is no joy left
In this transient world
For those who know
That soon their bodies
Shall waste away

Becoming an empty shell
Of white, creaking bones
Finally cast away
Like gourds in the cold autumnal wind.

Upon the foundations of bones
Plastered with the flesh and blood of creation
Is built a house
In which dwell
Pride, pretence, old age and death
And all the evils of worldly existence.

Just like the splendid chariot of a mighty king
Shining in the morning sunlight
With the intensity of pure gold
Loses its shine
With the passage of time
So also the body
Full of vigour in youth
Loses its beauty and strength
As it advances
From youth to old age
And upon death
Is nothing more
Than a handful of ashes.

But the goodness of your deeds
Does not age
Or wither away
It survives the onslaught
Of both old age and time.

A man who treads the path of falsehood and pleasure
Lives in ignorance
Not learning his lessons from life

As he remains in bondage
To error, hatred and greed
And while his wisdom does not grow
His body like that of an ox
Grows old and large.

Through endless rounds
Of births and deaths
Have I wandered
Looking in vain
For the builder of this house
Painful indeed is
Repeated birth and death
But now that I have seen you
Oh, house builder!
You shall not build this house again.

The house lies shattered
Its beams and domes broken
A heap of debris
Lying still upon the ground
As I delight in
The extinction of my thirst
For continual existence and becoming
And the emancipation of my mind
From sensual pleasures
And all selfish desires
As I taste the fruit of my labour
The eternal bliss of Nirvana.

Having spent their youth in idleness
Unrestrained and undisciplined
Squandering away their fortune
In pursuit of sensual pleasures
Instead of seeking the truth

And not having found it
The old pine for it
Like the crane pining away
In a lake without fish.

Like worn out bows
Lying discarded on the battlefield
Are those who have wasted their youth
Intoxicated by worldly pleasures
Totally unrestrained and undisciplined
And not having sought or found the truth
They tearfully look back
At the past
Sighing over it in their old age.

THE SELF

Vigilance is the way
To life eternal
If a man holds himself dearly
He should keep vigil
Over his thoughts, feelings and perceptions
His inner and outer states
During one of the three watches of the night.

Establish yourself in the Dhamma,
The eternal truth
Before you teach others
What is right and what is wrong
Just as the wise do
And you shall not suffer
The pain and suffering
Of earthly existence
In this life and after.

Before guiding others
Along the Path of Truth
Towards eternal deliverance
From evil
Turn towards yourself
And subdue

Your own thoughts and feelings
For the hardest
And most challenging task of all
Is the subduing of the self.

You are the Lord and master
Of yourself
Of your thoughts, feelings and perceptions
Bodily and mental states
Subdue and control them
And you shall then
Discover your master
Very hard to find
Who is none other
Than yourself.

By oneself
And no other
Is evil done
That lives on
In this cycle of birth and death
Crushing the evil-doer
Like the diamond
That crushes a hard stone.

Victory belongs to the enemy
Of the evil-doer
Whose wishes are fulfilled
When like the creeper
Overpowering the sal tree
The evil deeds of the doer
Trap and devour him
With the fire of evil
In this ocean of birth and death
Samsara.

Pleasurable to the senses
And easy
Are evil deeds
But alas!
They bring pain and suffering
To the doer
Unpleasant
And hard to do
Are good deeds
But they bring
Everlasting peace and happiness
To the doer.

Like the Khattaka reed
That bears the fruit
Of its own destruction
The foolish
Who scorn the words of wisdom
Of saints
And turn towards
The false doctrines of others
Bring about their own downfall
As they continue to suffer
The pain of continual rebirth
In this world of change and experience
Samsara.

By oneself are good and evil
Done and undone
By oneself is one injured
Good deeds bringing happiness
And evil deeds
Causing pain and suffering
To the doer
For in truth

Both purity and impurity
Belong to none other than ourselves
No one can purify another
The choice then
Is entirely ours.

Above all
Be dutiful
Realize your duty and perform it
Always
Never neglecting
Howsoever great the cause
Your duty
For the sake of another.

THE WORLD

This world of ours
Is shrouded in ignorance
And mysteries
Beyond our comprehension
Be wary then as you walk along
Taking care not to enter
The path of evil and pleasure
Do not be thoughtless
And take to worldly ways
And listen not to false doctrines
That keep you in bondage
To error, hatred and greed.

So arouse yourself
From your stupor
Do not be thoughtless
And tread joyfully
And steadfastly
Upon the Path of Truth
Drinking the sweet nectar of the Dhamma
And you shall dwell happily
In this life and after.

Abide not by the law of falsehood
But by the Law of Righteousness
And you shall dwell
Now and always
In peace and tranquillity
In this world and beyond.

Walk on
The Path of Righteousness
And you shall one day
Realize the ultimate reality
And then look upon this world
As a mirage
No more than an empty bubble
That bursts into the bottomless ocean
Of ignorance and slow time.

For then you shall know
That this world of ours
Is no more than
An illusion
Imperfect, impermanent and ever-changing
Without stability
And as you detach yourself
From this world of appearances
You escape the cycle of continuity
And enter
The borderless kingdom of righteousness
Where even the Lord of Death
Looks for you in vain.

Come and behold!
This beautiful world
Like a painted, royal chariot
That allures the foolish but not the wise

Who see through it
And having perceived the Dhamma
Remain detached from this world
And know
Like all things caused and conditioned
Imperfect, impermanent and ever-changing
It can never bring them
What they seek most
The eternal bliss of Nirvana.

And just like the moon
Emerging from behind the veil of clouds
Casts its silvery light on creation
So also the foolish man
Upon becoming wise
Illumines the world
With the golden light of truth.

And when the goodness in man
Overcomes his evil
He illumines this world
With his wisdom
Just like the moon
Breaking through the veil of clouds.

In this caused and conditioned
Dark and ignorant world
Few can see or perceive the truth
And indeed only a few
Find their way to heaven
Liberating themselves
From this web of worldliness
Like birds escaping the net.

Just like swans
Endowed with miraculous powers
Fly high into the sky
On the path of the sun
The wise transcend this world
Of joy and sorrow
And attain
The eternal bliss of Nirvana
Defeating Mara
And his forces of evil
With their weapons of righteousness.

He who violates the Dhamma
The moral law
Scoffs
And cares not for the life to come
Is given to evil ways
As he suffers
The pain of continual rebirth
In this world of change and experience
Samsara.

They are misers
Who find no joy
In giving what they have
To the poor and needy
To the hungry and distressed
And so
The doors of heaven
Shall remain closed to them.

But the wise
Who abide by the Dhamma
Their hearts full of charity
Boundless and unselfish

Who find no greater joy
Than giving what they have
To those in need
Shall live in happiness
Through the goodness of their deeds
Their karma
In this life and after.

Greater than the joy
Of absolute lordship
Of this earth and all the worlds
And entering the realm of the Gods
Is the joy of entering the tranquil waters
Of the stream that flows gently
Washing away our sins
As it carries us towards
The kingdom of righteousness
That is Nirvana.

THE BUDDHA

The greatest of all conquerors
Is he who has conquered the self
Whom the mightiest of conquerors
Can never conquer again
For he is the Buddha
Trackless and of infinite perception
Who is unreachable
Free from the net of desire and passion
And all conditioning
Beyond all description
The most enlightened of all beings
For he is the embodiment of the truth.

Even the lords emulate him
For he is the Buddha
The enlightened one
Whose mind is free
From evil and desire
And has become
The abode of the truth
Who delights in peace and meditation
And the unconditioned freedom
From the pain of rebirth.

A blessing it is
Though hard
To obtain human birth
Hard is the life of humans
Lost in a maze of thoughts
In this world
Of succession and change
Finding a way
To end the pain and suffering
Of earthly existence.

Harder still
Is to understand
The Dhamma
The eternal law
And abide by it
As we walk upon
The Path of Righteousness
But the hardest of all
Is sacrificing all that we desire
At the altar of the truth
In the attainment of the eternal bliss
Of Nirvana.

The Buddhas are the awakened ones
Whose words of wisdom teach us
That true bliss lies
In eschewing all that is evil
And perfecting the good within ourselves
Purifying and liberating our thoughts
From the bondage of error, hatred and greed
Killing the seed of desire in our minds
And illumining it
With the light of wisdom
That we may see the ultimate truth.

Be patient then
And endure the pain
Of worldly existence
In this cycle of continuity
Never veering
Howsoever great the cause
From the Path of Truth
Abide by the Dhamma
And you shall one day
Reach your final destination
Nirvana.

And you shall always
Make the Dhamma your guiding light
As you fight against Mara
And his forces of evil
In this battlefield of life
Never hurting or oppressing others
Finding faults in no one
Loving the unfortunate
Just as you love yourself
Meditating and practising moderation
In eating and sleeping
As you work tirelessly
Towards the welfare of all
For that indeed is
The sum of the Buddha's teachings.

A shower of gold coins
Cannot quench your thirst
For sensual pleasures
Or extinguish the fires of passion
Tormenting the mind
And wise indeed is the man
Who contemplates

The nature, arising and cessation of passion
And knows
That it only leads to sorrow
In this life and after.

There is no delight
In celestial or worldly pleasures
That can exceed
The delight of enlightenment
Of Nirvana
When desires are no more
And the illusion of self destroyed.

And he who delights
In the extinction
Of all desires
Is indeed a true follower
Of the Buddha.

The fearful
Run away from their fears
Seeking refuge in mountains and sacred trees
In forests and shrines
But alas!
Their fears follow them
Everywhere
And neither the mountains nor sacred trees
Forests nor shrines
Can bring comfort to their troubled minds
Or free them from their fears.

Those who seek refuge
Neither in mountains nor sacred trees
Forests nor sacred shrines
But in the Buddha – the awakened one

The Dhamma – the eternal law
The Sangha – the order of holy monks
The Four Noble Truths
Shall unfold before them
Illumining their minds
With the golden light of wisdom.

And they shall then perceive
With their enlightened minds
The nature and arising of suffering
And the Noble Eightfold Path
That leads to the cessation of suffering
And finally they shall
By believing and practisii
The Four Noble Truths
Attain salvation.

And remember
The Noble Eightfold Path
That leads to the island of peace and tranquillity
Nirvana
Amidst this ocean of birth and death
Is your best refuge
Enter it
And you shall be delivered.

A Buddha
An enlightened being
Is always hard to find
Who shines from afar
With the light of truth
And blessed are those
Amongst whom he is born
For wherever he is born
The household prospers.

Blessed is the Buddha
The awakened one
Blessed is the Dhamma
The eternal law
Blessed is the Sangha
The community of holy monks
Who continue to live
In peace and harmony
Their concord unbroken
In this world of succession and change.

And those who pay homage
To those worthy of it
To the Buddha and his disciples
Shall one day
Cross the river of sorrow and death
As they overcome all the forces of evil
And reach the island of eternal bliss
Uncaused and unconditioned
That is Nirvana.

HAPPINESS

There is no greater happiness
Than the happiness of freedom
From the bonds of error and hatred
So let us live happily
In freedom and without hatred
Amongst those who hate
Extending our love
Boundless and unselfish
To one and all.

There is no greater happiness
Than the happiness of freedom
From the inevitable pain
Of disease and decay
That attends birth
In this cycle of continuity
So let us live happily
And in freedom
Untouched by disease
Amongst the diseased.

There is no greater happiness
Than the happiness of freedom
From selfish attachments

To wealth and all things worldly
Impermanent and ever-changing
So let us live happily
Totally detached
Freeing ourselves from the anxiety
Of losing all that is ours
Amidst the ignorant and careworn
Attached to their worldly possessions
And all that is theirs
Who know not that in truth
Even they do not belong to themselves.

We who possess and desire nothing
Our hearts untainted by desire and greed
Not caring to hoard treasures
Amongst those who hoard
We shall live in ever-growing happiness
And shine from afar
Like the bright Gods
In the heavens above.

The conquest of lands
Rich and bountiful
Breeds hatred
Amongst the vanquished
Who dwell in sorrow
As the conqueror
Lives in anxiety
Fearing that the vanquished
May rise
And take all that is his
Turning his victory into defeat.

But he who has abandoned
All thoughts of victory and defeat

Lives happily
In peace and harmony.

Just as there is no fire
More furious than the fire of lust
And selfish passion
No disease more deadly
Than the disease of hatred and greed
No suffering more unbearable
Than the suffering of individuality
And separateness
There is no bliss
Higher than the bliss of Nirvana
Uncaused and unconditioned.

And just as there is no gift
Better than the gift of health
No wealth greater
Than the wealth of contentment
No kinsman more trustworthy
Than the Dhamma
There is no bliss higher
And more abiding
Than the bliss of Nirvana.

So drink
The sweet nectar of the Dhamma
As you meditate
And emancipate yourself
From fear and sin
And dwell evermore
In absolute bliss
Nirvana.

And bear in mind always
Walking the path of falsehood and pleasure
With the foolish
Can never bring you happiness
But company of the wise
Meeting or living with them
Leads to peace and happiness
As you walk along
The Path of Truth.

Vain and unprofitable
Is the company
Of the immature and foolish
No better than
Embarking upon a long journey
To damnation
With one's enemy
But the company
Of the wise
Treading with them
The path to freedom
Is always
As joyful as a family reunion.

So remember
Always live amongst
The wise
Who are full of understanding
Patient, responsible and noble
And above all who know
How to discern the right from the wrong
Follow in their footsteps
Like the moon
Follows the path of the stars
And everlasting happiness is yours.

PLEASURE

Be wary
Of the ways of the world
As you walk upon
The Path of Righteousness
And let not worldly pleasures
Distract your thoughts
From your goal
The truth.

And should you forget your goal
You will envy the happiness
Of those who meditate
So meditate
Upon your thoughts, feelings and perceptions
The Four Noble Truths
As you discipline your mind
And direct your thoughts
Towards the attainment of the ultimate truth
That is Nirvana.

The thirst for pleasure
Is insatiable
It never dies
But lives after us

Through countless births
And deaths
Creating attachment
To this world
Imperfect and impermanent
Leading to continual sorrow
In this cycle of continuity.

So liberate yourself
From this thirst
And detach yourself
From feelings perceived as pleasure and pain
And do not let yourself be pained
When you see the unpleasant
Or when you cannot see the pleasant
Transcend this world
Of duality and separateness
And attain the eternal bliss of Nirvana.

Transcend this world of duality and separateness
And live in freedom
Transcend all feelings of love and hate
Like and dislike
For the anxiety of cleaving
To feelings of loving and liking
To all those near and dear
Situations and experiences pleasant
Creates attachment
A fear of loss and grief
Leading only to suffering
In this life and after.

Happiness sought in fulfillment
Of sensual desires
Selfish and unprofitable

And passions of the mind, sensuousness and lust
Dies with the death of the objects of enjoyment
Creating a sense of loss and grief
For that which was and no longer exists
So, liberate yourself
From selfish desire and attachment
And attain the eternal bliss
Of Nirvana.

And bear in mind always,
Where there are selfish attachments
There is suffering and fear
So liberate yourself
From all selfish attachments
And you shall not suffer or fear.

Where there are selfish bonds
There is grief and fear
So, liberate yourself
From all selfish bonds
And you shall not grieve or fear.

Where there are selfish enjoyments
There is frustration and fear
Seek not selfish enjoyments
And you will be free
From frustration and fear.

Where there are selfish desires
There is anxiety and fear
Yield not to selfish desires
And you will be free
From anxiety and fear.

But for those
Who crave and ask for nothing
Who know that craving
Brings fear and pain
There is no fear, pain or frustration
For they are unselfish and detached.

So remember
He who is dutiful
And does his work
Abiding by the Dhamma
The eternal law
Who is pure
Who sees and speaks
Nothing but the truth
Endowed with wisdom and virtue
Him the world venerates and loves.

And he who is resolved in mind
With a heart untainted by desire
And all the evils of this world
Who longs for nothing more
Than the freedom from earthly desires
And attachments
In whom the desire to know
The ineffable truth has arisen
Who mindfully resists
The temptations of worldly existence
Is called the "uddhamsoto"
One who has entered the stream
That flows upwards
Towards the eternal bliss of Nirvana.

Just like the traveller
Who returns from a long and tiring journey

Is received
With love and joy
By all his kinsmen
So also your good deeds
Await and welcome you joyfully
Like your family and friends
With the promise
Of health, wealth and happiness
As you cross the river of death
From this life to the next.

ANGER

Liberate yourself
From all selfish desires
And worldly attachments
Renounce your anger
And your pride
And this transient world
Of name and form
Detach yourself
From all your belongings
As you walk upon
The Path of Truth
And you shall go beyond sorrow.

Anger is like the chariot
Uncontrolled
That has gone astray
On the battlefield
It clouds the mind
And hinders its progress
Along the Path of Righteousness
Towards the realization
Of the ultimate truth
Nirvana.

But he who learns to control his anger
Believing in and practising
The Four Noble Truths
Him I call the skillful charioteer
For he is in full control of the reins
While others
Merely hold them.

Let a man abide by the Dhamma
The eternal law
And overcome anger with kindness
Evil by good
Miserliness by liberality
And falsehood by truth.

Speak the truth
And be liberal
Always
Never resenting
Or yielding to anger
When asked for a little
Of what is yours
Rejoicing
In sharing what you have
With those who do not
For then only
Will you enter the world of Gods
Before entering
The gates of immortality
That is Nirvana.

They are wise
Who are self-controlled
And harm no one
As they walk along

The Path of Righteousness
Striving for the ultimate truth
Ever-mindful
Of their thoughts, feelings and perceptions
Meditating night and day
Upon the Four Noble Truths
They enter the borderless state
Of peace and tranquility
Beyond the realms of sorrow and death
That is Nirvana.

There is an ancient saying
"Blamed are those who remain silent,
Blamed are those who talk too much,
Blamed are those who talk in moderation."

There is indeed none
In this world
Who escapes the suffering of blame.

There never was
In the remote past
Nor will there ever be
In the unforeseeable future
Nor is there in the present
Anyone who is
Entirely praiseworthy
Or blameworthy.

But those who are wise
Pure and good
Endowed with wisdom and virtue
Who find joy in meditation
Shine with the brilliance of a pure gold coin
Are praised by one and all

In the worlds of Gods and men
They are praised by the greatest of Gods
The Lord Brahma himself – The Creator.

Be mindful
Always
Of your body
And physical states
As you practise self-restraint
And control your physical desires
For then
You slowly
Train you body
To abide by the Dhamma
The moral law
As you expiate all its sins.

Be mindful
Always
Of what you speak
And speak not
Harsh or angry words
As you abstain from lying
Slander and abuse
And all the evils of speech
But do not restrain yourself
From speaking softly and gently
Words of wisdom
From the unfathomable depths of truth.

Be mindful
Always
Of your mind
And skillfully control your thoughts
Cultivating only

Thoughts of love
And compassion
Purged of desire, ill-will and greed
As you discipline your mind
Along the Path of Truth.

And do not fail to destroy
And prevent the arising
Of thoughts that are evil
And slowly
With a mind that is pure
Make yourself an island of truth
In this ocean of birth and death
Samsara.

Wise indeed are those
Who are self-controlled
Who abstain
From the evils of the mind, body and speech
As they walk along
The Path of Truth
Liberating themselves
From the web of selfish desires
And attachments
As they dwell happily
In peace and tranquillity
In this world of change and experience
Samsara.

IMPURITY

You are like the leaf
Withered and dry
Waiting to be blown away
By the cold, winter's wind
To an unknown land.

And as the messengers of death
Stand before you
You wait silently at the threshold of departure
Without vitality
Unprepared for the journey
You are about to undertake
Upon the river of death.

Hasten
Before it is too late
And as you stand
At the threshold of death
Become an island of truth unto yourself
In this ocean of birth and death
And strive hard to attain wisdom
Along the Path of Righteousness
Purge your thoughts of all defilements
Become innocent and pure

For then you shall
Enter the gates of heaven
And dwell amongst the elect.

You are now in the presence of Yama
The King of Death
There is no time for rest
And you are so unprepared
For your journey
So light the lamp of truth within
And make an island of peace for yourself
In this ocean of birth and death
Samsara.

Strive hard to attain wisdom
Along the Path of Truth
Extinguish all selfish desires
Completely
Purge your mind
Of all its impurities
Become innocent and pure
And you will be liberated
From this painful cycle
Of birth and death.

Just like the silversmith
Painstakingly
Removes the dust from silver
Little by little
And purifies it
So must you slowly
Purge your thoughts
Of egotism, anger and hatred
And all the impurities of the mind
Extinguishing all selfish desires

That cause becoming and re-existence
In this cycle of continuity
Samsara.

Just as iron is corroded
Gradually by rust
That it breeds
So also the evil deeds that you do
Which bring you momentary pleasure
Shall slowly devour you
Leading you on the path of evil
And destruction.

Just as sacred verses
When not chanted
Lose their efficacy
A house in disrepair
And neglected
Falls to ruins
A body when not exercised
Loses its health and vigour
So, also a vigilant man
Who whilst walking the Path of Truth
Loses his vigilance
Fails to attain the unconditioned bliss
And freedom of Nirvana.

Impurities
Born out of selfish desire
Pervade this entire world
They are here, there and everywhere
They are seen amongst women
Immodest and undignified
Amongst men
Who lack generosity

And resent what they give
But the greatest impurity of all
Is ignorance
That enslaves you to thirst
Egotism and greed.

Selfish deeds bring no happiness
Here and hereafter
So strive for the ultimate truth
Purge your mind
Of all impurities
As you tread the Path of Righteousness
And attain the supreme wisdom
That liberates you
From the fetters of ignorance
And you shall then dwell in purity.

Easy is the life of those who tread
The path of evil and pleasure
Who are without shame and crow like
Who seek satisfaction
In creating mischief all around
Not caring or aspiring for the truth
Impudent and dissolute
Who expend their energies
Indulging in momentary pleasures
Harming others and themselves as well
They are fools who do not know
That the evil they do
Shall one day recoil on them.

Hard is the life of the humble, kind and detached
Who strive earnestly towards perfection
Moral and intellectual
As they extinguish

All feelings of selfish desire and attachment
As they walk along
The Path of Truth
Earnestly trying to live
A life of purity.

So discipline your mind
And meditate upon
Your thoughts, feelings and perceptions
As you abstain
From the evils of killing and lying
Stealing, adultery and drunkenness
And remember
By indulging in these evils
You dig your own grave
As you continue to exist
In this cycle of continuity
Samsara.

And bear in mind
An undisciplined mind
Leads to evil
That shall one day
Rebound on you
So do not let greed and vice
Bring you lingering grief
As it leads you on the path of falsehood and pleasure.

So be happy and content
With what you have
Giving out of faith
And affection
What is yours
Never envying or resenting
Gifts that are given to others

For if you do
Your thoughts remain tormented
By feelings of envy
As you pray in vain
For a restful sleep
And the enjoyment
Of a peaceful state of mind.

So meditate
As you walk upon the Path of Truth
And dig out
The roots of envy
And you shall enjoy
Lasting peace and tranquillity
In this life and after.

There is indeed no snare
More deadly than delusion
No fire more furious
Than the fire of lust
No jailer stronger
Than hate
And no torrent more powerful
Than the torrent of greed.

And those who realize these truths
Emancipate their minds
From the fetters of ignorance
As they experience
The bliss of enlightenment
That is Nirvana.

Easy and pleasurable it is
To find faults in others
Winnowing them like chaff

As we turn away from our own
And skillfully hide them
Like a cheat hiding an unlucky draw.

And if we dwell
On the faults of others
Instead of our own
Then our passions and desires
Shall grow and with time
Eat into the goodness of our deeds
Making our minds
The abode of evil.

There is no path in the sky
And there is no refuge
On land or the high seas
Or anywhere in this universe
For those driven by selfish desires
But the disciples of the Buddha
Liberating their minds
From all selfish desires and attachments
Live in the unconditioned bliss
And freedom of Nirvana.

There is no path in the sky
And indeed there is no refuge in this world
On land or the high seas
For those driven by selfish desires
But the disciples of the Buddha
Know that in reality
This world of ours
Is imperfect and ever-changing
And so, they dwell happily
Unattached and unshaken
In this world of change and experience
Samsara.

THE PERSON ESTABLISHED IN THE DHAMMA

Those who do not abide by the Dhamma
The moral law
And resort to violent
Or unjust means
To achieve their ends
Shall suffer the evil of their misdeeds
In this life and after.

But those who abide by the Dhamma
The eternal law
And know how to discern
The right from the wrong
As they lead others
Upon the Path of Truth
Never resorting
Howsoever great
Or grievous the cause
To violence or unjust means
In achieving their ends
They are truly enlightened
The guardians of the Dhamma.

It is not the number of words you speak
Nor the number of books you read

That make you learned
But your thoughts
Tranquil and free from selfish desire
Hatred and fear
Established in the Dhamma
The all-pervasive truth
That make you learned.

It is not talking about the Dhamma
That makes you an upholder
Of the truth
But abiding by it
By believing and practising
The Four Noble Truths
Even if you are a little learned
As you extinguish all selfish desires
In your mind
And learn to live
In peace and harmony.

It is not the number of grey hairs you have
Or your years
That make you an elder
But your thoughts and deeds
And the years spent
In contemplation of the Four Noble Truths
Practising self-control
In overcoming selfish desires
And evils
Of the mind, body and speech
Whilst treading the Path of Righteousness
That make you an elder.

A true elder is he
Who is ever-truthful

Self-controlled and gentle
Non-violent and virtuous
Whose mind purged
Of all selfish desires, hatred and greed
Has become the habitation of the truth.

The beauty of a person
Lies not in his outward appearance
In the perfection of his form and complexion
Refinement of manner or grace
Or the utterance of pleasant words
Hollow and meaningless
But in his intrinsic worth
In the nobility of his character
And the purity of his thoughts
Devoid of selfish desires
Jealousy and deceit
Freed from thirst
And worldly attachments.

Beautiful then
Are only those who have destroyed
Completely
All feelings of envy, hatred and wickedness
From the very roots
Who are without guilt
Gentle and wise
And have drunk the sweet nectar
Of the Dhamma
The eternal law.

Shaving of the head
Does not make you
Whose thoughts are governed by selfish desires
A monk

For you are undisciplined and untrue
In both thought and deed.

Remember
A true monk is he
Who has disciplined his mind
By extinguishing all fires of passion
Hatred and greed
Treading the Path of Righteousness
Liberating it from selfish desires
Large and small
And establishing it in the eternal truth
The Dhamma.

Begging for alms
Does not make you
Whose thoughts are unchaste
A bhikku
It is only those
Who abide by the Dhamma
Completely
And not partially
Whose thoughts are purged
Of anger, hatred and greed
And all impurities
Who are true bhikkus.

And remember always
It is only those
Who work ceaselessly
Towards the destruction
Of the illusion of self
That it may no longer exist
Who go through life detached
Beyond both good and evil
Who indeed are true bhikkus.

The observance of silence
Does not make those
Who are ignorant and immature
Sages
For their thoughts rooted in evil
And falsehood
Burning with the fires
Of envy, hatred and greed
Cannot perceive the eternal truth
The Dhamma.

It is in only those
Who by treading the Path of Righteousness
Have perceived the Dhamma
Who holding the scales of justice
Choose the good over the bad
Whom I call sages.

And remember
Those who aspire for nobility
Seeking happiness by injuring
Living creatures
Great and small
Can never be noble
It is only those
Who live peacefully
Abiding by the Dhamma
The eternal law
Harming no one
Howsoever great or small
Who are truly noble.

Indeed
Inefficacious are rituals and resolutions
Learning and celibacy

And even meditation
In the attainment of Nirvana
And it is only those
Who have utterly extinguished
Every selfish desire
The thirst for sensual pleasures
Existence and non-existence
Who attain the unconditioned bliss
And freedom of Nirvana.

THE EIGHTFOLD PATH

Of all the paths
The Noble Eightfold Path
Of righteousness and virtue
That leads
To the emancipation of the mind
From the fetters
Of selfish desires
And all the evils
Of worldly existence
Is the best.

Of all the truths
The Four Noble Truths
The belief and practice
Of which
Lead to enlightenment
And release
From the pain and suffering
Of continual birth and death
Is the best.

Of all the mental states
The state of detachment
That leads

To the subduing of passions
And worldly desires
Is the best.

And of all the human beings
The awakened one
Who by uttering
Words of wisdom
From the immeasurable depths of truth
Shows us the way to salvation
Is the best.

This is the path
There indeed is no other
Here or anywhere in the universe
Or outside it
That leads to the cessation of sorrow
And the eternal bliss of Nirvana.

It is only the Eightfold Path of Righteousness
That leads to the purging of your mind
Of all selfish desires and défilements
Empowering you
With the weapon of your wisdom
As you battle Mara
And his forces of evil
Destroying them completely
As you enter the gates of immortality
Nirvana.

This was the path
I trod and made known
Conquering Mara and his evil forces
With the power of truth
As the arrows of sorrow

Fell away from me
And all my suffering came to an end
I reached
The borderless and formless
Kingdom of righteousness
That is Nirvana.

The effort and choice
Is finally yours
It is you who have to strive
Tirelessly
As you walk upon the Path of Truth
Towards the realization
Of the ultimate reality
And remember
The Buddhas
Merely show you the way
Towards salvation.

So follow this path and meditate
Upon your thoughts, feelings and perceptions
Liberate yourself from selfish desires
And the bondage of Mara
As you fight against the tide of worldliness
And reach the tranquil shores of Nirvana.

When you meditate
And attain the supreme wisdom
You realize
That all things created
Are transitory
They arise and pass away
And that the only reality
Is the eternal bliss of Nirvana
You liberate yourself

From sorrow and suffering
Having trod the Eightfold Path
The way to purity and wisdom.

Those who realize
That all creation
And created beings
Are full of sorrow
Free themselves from suffering
As they see at last
The ultimate truth
Having trod the Eightfold Path
The way to purity and wisdom.

There is in reality
No self
Within or outside the individual
Or anywhere in the universe
Or outside it
The idea of self
Is merely an illusion
That binds you
To selfish desire
And all the evils of worldly existence
And those who realize it
Attain pure wisdom
Treading the Eightfold Path of Righteousness
For this indeed is the path to unconditioned bliss and freedom.

Arouse yourself
From your stupor
Now
When you are young and strong
And embark upon
The journey to salvation

Tread the Eightfold Path of Righteousness
Towards enlightenment
And you shall be delivered.

And should you be weak and waver
Unresolved in mind
Giving in to sloth
And the fulfillment of sensual pleasures
You shall lose your way
To Nirvana
And the attainment of the supreme wisdom
As you remain in bondage
To error and worldly attachments
In this cycle of continuity
Samsara.

Guard your thoughts
Words and deeds
Always
Tread the Path of Truth
Overcoming all selfish desires and attachments
For your guarded thoughts
Words and deeds
Shall lead you one day
Towards the attainment of pure wisdom.

Remember
Meditation and the Eightfold Path
Is the way
Followed by the righteous
That leads to wisdom and self-liberation
Lack of meditation
And divergence from the Eightfold Path
Is the way
Followed by the fools
That leads to sorrow, death and destruction.

So knowing the path that leads to deliverance
And the path that leads to sorrow
Choose the Eightfold Path to wisdom
For you shall then drink the sweet nectar
Of the Dhamma
As you liberate yourself
From the pain and suffering
Of continual rebirth.

Fell all the trees
The entire forest of selfish desires
That obstruct
The golden light of truth
From entering your mind
And illumining your thoughts
Destroy them completely
Each and every one of them
And you shall be on your way to liberation.

Extinguish
Every trace of lust
In your mind
That binds you
To the pain and suffering
Of continual rebirth
Like the suckling calf
That is bound
To its mother the cow.

Destroy every selfish desire
And urge
With your weapons of righteousness
Pluck them out
As you would

With you hands
Pluck out an autumn lotus
From the depths of slime
And look to no one
But the wise man
Who knows the way
To salvation.

Follow him
On the Path of Truth
And you shall reach
The unageing, deathless and formless state
That is Nirvana.

Think not
Of your yesterdays and tomorrows
But dwell in the present
Think not
Of making your winter home
Your summer or monsoon homes
And lose yourself
In such thoughts
For they are all
A part of this transient world.

Think instead
Of the intransient
Of your final goal and abode
The uncaused and unconditioned
Kingdom of righteousness
Nirvana.

Just as a flood
Comes and carries away
A sleeping village

So also
Death comes
And carries off the man
Absorbed in his possessions
His cattle and sons
And all his worldly possessions
Whose mind distracted by worldly pleasures
Has alas!
Not perceived the truth
All-pervasive and eternal.

Bear in mind
Neither your parents
Nor your children
Can rescue you
From the cruel hands of death
So hasten
And follow the Path of Truth
That leads to enlightenment
And emancipation
From the cycle
Of birth and death.

VARIED VERSES

Wise indeed is the man
Who knows how to discern
The right from the wrong
Who when he beholds
A greater happiness
Abandons the desire
For seeking the lesser
And goes instead for the greater
Abiding happiness
In this life and after.

Those who build their happiness
Upon the sorrows of others
Get caught
In the inescapable web of evil and hatred
As they continue to suffer
The evil of their misdeeds
In this cycle of birth and death
Samsara.

Those who care not
For the Dhamma
The moral law
Who fail to do

What ought to be done
And do not fail to do
What ought not to be done
Carry with them
The burden of their misdeeds
That continues to grow
As they tread the path of falsehood and pleasure.

Those who abide by the Dhamma
The moral law
Who never fail to do
What ought to be done
And fail to do
What ought not to be done
Meditating
Upon the Four Noble Truths
Self-controlled and compassionate
As they tread the Path of Truth
Shall one day
Go beyond realms of sorrow and suffering.

I beseech ye
To kill mother lust
And father pride
And all the kings of carnal pleasures
To tread the Path of Truth
Towards the kingdom of righteousness
And you shall be delivered.

He indeed is the true Brahmin
The truthful one
Who treading the Path of Righteousness
Has killed mother lust
And father pride
And all the kings of carnal pleasures

Annihilating the ego
That obstructs his path to the truth
Who goes unscathed
As he overcomes ignorance
And is delivered from evil.

Wide awake
And vigilant
Are the disciples of the Buddha
Whose thoughts flow tirelessly
Towards the light of truth
And remain focused night and day
On their master
The Buddha.

Wide awake
And vigilant
Are the disciples of the Buddha
Whose thoughts flow tirelessly
Towards the light of truth
And remain focused night and day
Upon the Dhamma
The eternal law.

Wide awake
And vigilant
Are the disciples of the Buddha
Whose thoughts flow tirelessly
Towards the light of truth
And remain focused night and day
Upon the Sangha
The holy order of monks.

Wide awake
And vigilant

Are the disciples of the Buddha
Whose thoughts flow tirelessly
Towards the light of truth
And remain focused on their body
And physical states
Night and day
As they tread the Path of Truth.

Wide awake
And vigilant
Are the disciples of the Buddha
Whose thoughts flow tirelessly
Towards the light of truth
Delighting night and day
In the cultivation of compassion
And the destruction of all selfish desires
Hatred and greed.

Wide awake
And vigilant
Are the disciples of the Buddha
Whose thoughts flow tirelessly
Towards the light of truth
Delighting night and day
In the bliss of meditation.

Painful it is
Living the life of a recluse
Or a wanderer
Painful it is
Living in this world with the worldly
Painful is the life of a householder
And painful indeed is
Repeated existence
In this cycle of continuity
Samsara.

So walk on the Path of Truth
Towards your ultimate goal
Nirvana
And you shall be released
From the pain and suffering
Of worldly existence.

Those whose thoughts
Purged of all evil
Are rooted in the truth
Who are noble
In thought, word and deed
Are honoured
Wherever they go
By one and all.

And like the snowy peaks
Of the mighty Himalayas
The noble ones
Shine from afar
Radiating the light of truth
Wherever they go
While those
Whose thoughts
Are clouded by ignorance
Go unnoticed
Like the arrow shot
In the darkness of the night.

Beware of the ways of the world
And yield not to indolence
As you walk upon the Path of Truth
Act alone
Sit alone
Sleep alone

Subdue your passions
And abiding joy is yours
When you have conquered your ego
And extinguished all traces
Of selfish desires
Liberating yourself
From the painful cycle
Of birth and death.

THE DOWNWARD COURSE

He who does not speak the truth
And he who denies his actions
Mental and physical
Are governed by evil thoughts
That lead them
On the downward course to hell.

Both are partners in evil
And they shall continue to suffer
In the darkness of their ignorance
In this life and after.

Those who wear the yellow robe
Uncontrolled and ill-behaved
Their thoughts full of selfish desires
That chain them
To the wheel of individuality
Enter the downward course to hell
And continue to suffer
The pain of repeated births
In this cycle of continuity
Samsara.

It is better then
For the monk
Who is uncontrolled and untrue
To swallow a ball
Of red, hot molten iron
Than to live a life
Of deceit
On the alms of the faithful.

Pleasurable it is
To commit adultery
Enjoying the company
Of another's wife
In secrecy
But alas!
The excitement of adultery
Dies down
As the Law of Karma prevails
And one suffers feelings of anxiety
Loss of sleep and condemnation
And the guilt and remorse
Of flouting the Dhamma
The moral law.

The short-lived pleasure
Of treading the downward course of evil
Committing adultery
With another man's wife
Brings pain and suffering
For there is indeed no peace or happiness
Or the accumulation of good karma
For the frightened lying in the arms of the frightened.

Just as a blade of grass
Wrongly held
Cuts the finger
So also
Those ascetics
Who do not discriminate
The right from the wrong
While practising asceticism
Their thoughts full of selfish desire
Bring suffering upon themselves
In this life and after
As they embark upon
The downward course.

Be sincere and genuine
In all your efforts
And above all
Be true to yourself
As you perform your duty
Resolutely
Never veering from the Path of Truth.

Break no vows
And abide by the code of chastity
And you shall be rewarded
In this life and after.

And remember
Like the careless ascetic
Who smears himself
With more and more dust
Those who waver
And half-heartedly perform their duty
Gather the dust

Of their bad karma
That clings to them
Ever so firmly
In this world and beyond.

Guard yourself
Like a fortress
Within and without
From the hidden dangers
Of worldly pleasures
Strive along the Path of Truth
And do not waste a moment
Of your precious time
For those moments lost
Shall send you on the downward course
As you continue to suffer
In this cycle of rebirth
Samsara.

They indeed are fools
Who are ashamed of deeds
They should be proud of
And proud of deeds
They should be ashamed of
Fearful when they should not fear
And fearless when they should fear
For they follow false doctrines
And cannot discern
The right from the wrong
As they blindly enter
The downward course.

But those
Who abide by the Dhamma
The eternal truth

As they mindfully meditate
Upon the Four Noble Truths
Know how to discern
The good from the evil
And the right from the wrong
For they follow true doctrines
And enter
The upward Path of Righteousness
Towards salvation.

THE ELEPHANT

Just as the elephant
Patiently endures
The pain and suffering
Of the arrows
Shot at him
Upon the battlefield
So shall I
Patiently endure
The pain and suffering
Of harsh words
Spoken by the unkind
For I know
That more often than not
People are inconsiderate.

And so I stand unperturbed
Upon the battlefield of life
Working my way
Upon the Path of Truth
Towards salvation.

It is not the rogue
But the tamed elephant
Who goes to the battlefield

Carrying the king
And patiently endures the pains
Inflicted by the weapons of war
And just like the tamed elephant
The best among men is he
Who trains his thoughts
To abide by the Dhamma
As he meditates
Upon the Four Noble Truths
And patiently endures
Harsh words spoken by the unkind
As he marches silently
Towards the kingdom of righteousness.

Of all the animals
Upon this creation
Trained mules are good
Even better are Sindhi horses and mighty elephants
But amongst men there is none better
Than the man
Whose well-trained mind
As he walks along the Path of Truth
Leads him to victory
Upon the battlefield of life
As he dwells
In the unconditioned bliss
And freedom
Of Nirvana.

And bear in mind always
No animal can carry you
Across the river
Of sorrow and suffering
To the untrodden land of Nirvana
It is only a well trained mind

Purged of all evil
That can lead you
To this state of eternal bliss
Beyond all description, space and time
That is Nirvana.

The mighty elephant Dhanapalka
Is hard to control
For when in rut and bound
He does not eat
Pining away for his mate
In the elephant grove.

Those who do not exert themselves
As they walk along the Path of Truth
Distracted by
The path of evil and pleasure
Who are given to gluttony
And excessive sleep
Fail to reach
Their ultimate destination
Nirvana
And continue to suffer
The pain of repeated existence
In this cycle of continuity
Samsara.

A long time ago
My mind uncontrolled
And undisciplined
Wandered aimlessly
Wherever it pleased
Like yours
But now
I control my mind

As I train it
To abide by the Dhamma
The eternal law
Just like the mahout
Who with his hooked staff
Controls the elephant.

Just like the elephant
With all its strength
Pulls itself
Out of the mud
And does not sink
So must you
Be ever-vigilant
As you guard your mind
Against impure thoughts
Pulling yourself out
Of the eddy of unrighteous behaviour
And evil ways.

If ever you find
Someone good, loving and wise
Befriend him
And walk with him
Along the Path of Truth
Overcoming all the dangers of earthly existence
And you shall one day realize
The ultimate truth
As you liberate yourself
From the endless cycle
Of birth and death.

And if
You fail to find a friend
Who is wise, gentle and honest

Then walk alone
Like a king
Who has renounced his kingdom
Or the elephant
Who roams freely in the forest
For it is better
And more profitable
To be alone
Than to seek
The company of fools
Who lead you
On the path of evil and pleasure
Towards destruction.

So be happy and content
With what you have
Commit no sin
Or give in to evil ways
Walk alone
Along the Path of Truth
Like the elephant in the forest.

Friendship when mutual
Is always
Pleasant and satisfying
It is the sharing
Of one's joys and sorrows
And all the experiences
Of earthly existence.

Better still
Is the friendship of good deeds
That endure
The endless cycle of birth and death
But happiest is he

Who has gone beyond the realms
Of sorrow and death.

The happiness of parenthood
Of being a mother
Or a father
Or one who abides by the Dhamma
The moral law
Is undoubtedly great
But the greatest happiness of all
Is that experienced by the illumined sage
Whose mind freed from the fetters of worldly existence
And selfish desires
Has become
The abode of the truth.

And remember always
A life of virtue
Faith in the eternal Dhamma
And the attainment of the highest wisdom
When your mind purged of all impurities
Is illumined by the eternal light of truth
Will bring you lasting joy.

THIRST

The thoughtless
Who neither desire
Nor care to know
The truth
Are always
Driven by selfish desires
Fierce and untrained
Which like a creeper growing wild
Jump from one life to another
Like monkeys
Searching in vain
For fruits in the forest.

Beware,
Before your desires
Fierce and uncontrolled
Drive you
To destinations unknown
As your sorrows like wild grass
After the rains spread
So, before it is too late
Conquer your desires
Before they devour you
As you walk upon

The Path of Righteousness
And behold!
How like tiny drops of water
Falling off the lotus leaf
All your sorrows
Fall away.

I exhort you
Gathered before me
To destroy
Once and for all
The root of craving
And all selfish desires
Just as you would
Uproot the birana grass
That Mara may never again
Crush you
Like the stream
That crushes
The reeds
Growing upon its banks.

Like the felled tree
Lying lifeless
Its roots undestroyed
Growing firmly in the ground
Grows again
So also
Your sorrows
Visit you again
If your desires
Fierce and uncontrolled
Are not extinguished
Once and for all.

As the thirty six streams
Of the thoughtless
Flow broad and strong
From the mind
Towards pleasure
The tide of passion
Sweeps them away
From the Path of Truth
Into the ocean of suffering.

Powerful are these streams
That flow everywhere
Misguiding you
Upon the path of evil and pleasure
So remember
If ever you see
The creeper of passion
Invading your thoughts
Uproot it
With the strength of your wisdom
Before it overwhelms you.

And bear in mind
That we are humans
Mere mortals
Our thoughts governed
By thirst for sensual pleasures
And subject to worldly attachments
So be wary
For powerful indeed
Are these attachments and pleasures
That carry us
Through endless rounds
Of births and deaths

In this cycle of continuity
Samsara.

How like the hunted hare
You continue to exist
Through countless births
Pursued relentlessly
By the evil forces of selfish desire
That bind you
To this wheel of individuality
And you continue to suffer
For a long, long time
So liberate yourself
From this selfish thirst
And enjoy the unconditioned freedom of Nirvana.

Behold!
How those who emerge free
From the forest of selfish desires
Into the clearing
Are driven into another
Of darkness and despair
Where they remain again
Through many births
In bondage to error and hatred.

There is no fetter
Say the wise
In this caused and conditioned
World of ours
Not even the fetters of iron, wood or rope
Stronger and more powerful
Than that of selfish attachment
To jewels, sons and wives
That bind you

To repeated existence
In this cycle of continuity
Samsara.

Break through the fetters
Of selfish desires
In your mind
Turn away once and for all
From this world of sensual pleasure
And you shall
Transcend this caused and conditioned world
As you enter the state of eternal bliss
Unageing and formless
That is Nirvana.

Bear in mind
You are no better
Than a spider
Caught in its own web
So before it is too late
Liberate yourself
From your web of evil
By the goodness of your deeds
And as you turn away from this world
Of sensual pleasure and sorrow
You shall dwell
In unconditioned freedom
Nirvana.

And if you want to reach
The tranquil shores of Nirvana
As you walk along the Path of Truth
Give up completely
All that there is
Before you,

Behind and the in the middle
Liberate your mind
From all selfish desires
And attachments
And you shall then
Cross the river of passion
And go beyond birth and death.

Let not doubts
Passions and cravings
Strengthen the fetters of worldly existence
If you want to cross this river of sorrow
And reach
The deathless shores of Nirvana
Meditate upon your inner and outer states
And the Four Noble Truths
As you discriminate between
The permanent and impermanent
The pleasant and unpleasant
And liberate yourself
From the evil forces of Mara
And the endless cycle
Of birth and death.

He who is fearless
And without sin
In whom the thirst
For sensual pleasure
And existence
Has been extinguished
Utterly
Who has through the goodness of his deeds
Removed every thorn from his life
Transcending good and evil
This is indeed
His last body.

He who has extinguished
Every selfish desire
And craving for separate existence
Freeing himself from all attachments
And attained the supreme wisdom
Who has comprehended at last
All the words
And their meanings
He knows all
There is to know
This indeed
Is his last body.

Having conquered all
And myself
I dwell now
In the timeless realm of purity
And freedom
That is Nirvana
And having renounced this world
Destroying every selfish desire
I have become a light unto myself
I am my own Lord and master
My own teacher
Whom shall I then
Call my teacher?

There is indeed
No better gift
Sweeter and more joyful
Than the Dhamma
The eternal truth
That quietens the mind
And ends

Once and for all
All earthly cravings
And the accompanying sorrow
As we dwell in purity and bliss
Nirvana.

Be wary then
As you guard your wealth
For it harms the greedy
Those of little understanding
But not the righteous
Who seek not pleasures
Of the "here and now"
As they strive along
The Path of Truth
Towards their ultimate goal
Nirvana.

Just like weeds
Make their way silently
Destroying
The lush green fields
That lie yonder
Greed enters
And disturbs the mind
With thoughts of possessions
And wealth
Of me and mine
Leading you on the path of evil
So I beseech ye
Before it is too late
Pay homage
To the righteous
Who are without greed

And you shall then
Dwell in happiness.

Just like weeds
That make their way silently
Destroying
The lush green fields
That lie yonder
Lust enters
And disturbs the mind
Kindling the desire
For sensual pleasures
Leading you on the path of evil
So I beseech ye
Before it is too late
Pay homage to the righteous
Who are without lust
For you shall then
Dwell in happiness.

Just like weeds make their way silently
Destroying
The lush green fields
That lie yonder
Hatred enters
And disturbs the mind
With thoughts of
War and revenge
Leading you on the path of evil
So I beseech ye
Before it is too late
Pay homage to the righteous
Who are without hatred
For you shall then
Dwell in happiness.

Just as weeds make their way silently
Destroying
The lush green fields
That lie yonder
Selfish desires arise
And disturb the mind
With thoughts of
Egotism, anger and jealousy
Leading you on the path of evil
So I beseech ye
Before it is too late
Pay homage to the righteous
In whom
All selfish desires have been expunged
For you shall then
Dwell in happiness.

THE BHIKKU

Remember always
Self restraint
Of the senses
Of the eyes and ears
Tongue and nose
Is the path
To eternal bliss
And the cessation of suffering
Nirvana.

Those who discipline
Their bodies
Speech and thoughts
In accordance with the Dhamma
The eternal law
Shall emancipate themselves
From the fetters
Of worldly existence
And shall one day go beyond sorrow
As they enter the gates
Of the kingdom of righteousness
Nirvana.

He indeed
Is the true bhikku
Who has disciplined
His hands and feet
And speech
In selfless service of others
Well controlled in all he does and says
He delights in meditation
And the tranquillity of his thoughts.

He shall one day
Go beyond sorrow
And be freed from this cycle
Of birth and death.

He indeed
Is the true bhikku
Who speaks gently
Uttering words of wisdom
That explain the Dhamma
The eternal law
And abides by it
Always
Who is free from pride
Finding joy in solitude
And meditation upon the Dhamma
Virtuous and wise
He never falls away from the truth.

He indeed
Is a true bhikku
Who is content
With what he has
Never envying
What others have

And so he rejoices
Meditating on the Dhamma
The eternal law
And in the tranquillity of his thoughts.

Peace and happiness
Elude the bhikku
Who envies all
That others have
Not content with what is his
He struggles in vain
Along the Path of Truth.

Even the Gods
Praise the bhikku
Who is happy and content
With what he has
In whom the desire to possess
People and things
Has been extinguished
Utterly
Who grieves not
Over what he does not possess
Who lives in purity and rejoices
In selfless service to those around.

And he indeed
Is the true bhikku
Who lives in peace and joy
Friendly with one and all
With faith in the doctrine
Of the Buddha
The blessed one
And he shall one day
Be delivered

As he reaches
The island of eternal peace and joy
Nirvana.

Oh! Bhikku!
Empty your boat
Of all your burdens
Of repeated existence
Extinguish your hatred
And all your passions
In this ocean of birth and death
That your boat may float lightly
Towards the island of eternal bliss
Nirvana.

Bhikku! I beseech you!
Cut off once and for all
The fetters of worldly existence
Overcome the five hindrances
Of egotism, doubt, folly
Lust and hatred
Rid yourself of the five evils
The longing for rebirth
With and without form
Your self-will, vanity and ignorance
And develop the five qualities
Of faith, courage
Mindfulness, meditation and wisdom
That you may cross the river of death
And reach the deathless shores of Nirvana.

Oh, bhikku!
Do not neglect your duty
And run after sensual pleasures
Meditate

Upon your thoughts, feelings and perceptions
And the Four Noble Truths
As you guard your thoughts from straying
From the Path of Truth
So that you may never
Swallow the red hot iron ball
And cry out in agony
"This is suffering!"

Remember always
Vain and inefficacious
Is meditation without wisdom
And there is indeed no wisdom
For those who do not meditate
It is only
Wisdom attained through meditation
That draws you closer
Towards the distant
Silvery shores of Nirvana.

And when a bhikku
Stays the stream of thought
And stills his mind
As he walks upon
The Path of Righteousness
He enters
An empty house
And all at once
His heart fills
With divine joy
Born out of
The right discernment
Of the Dhamma
The eternal law.

The bhikku
Who treads the path of virtue
And meditates
Upon the Four Noble Truths
Purges his mind
Of its impurities
And comprehends
The nature, origin and destruction
Of the elements of his body
As he realizes
The ultimate truth
And experiences the bliss of immortality
Nirvana.

Have faith
In the doctrine of the blessed one
Oh Bhikku!
Train your senses
As you abide by the Dhamma
And befriend only those
Who are pure and noble
Create no enemies
Loving others
Just as you love yourself
Perform your duties well
And you shall then
Live in ever-growing happiness
And put an end to your sufferings.

Just as the varsika plant
Sheds its withered flowers
So should you
Shed all your passions
Hatred and greed
For he indeed is a true bhikku

Who is calm
In thought, word and deed
Who has established himself
In the Dhamma
The eternal truth
And turned away from the allurements
Of this world of sensual pleasures.

Remember bhikku
To seek the truth
Within yourself
Be self reliant
Always
As you strive along
The Path of Righteousness.

So rouse yourself
And meditate upon
Your thoughts, feelings and perceptions
Be vigilant and examine yourself
As you guard your thoughts
Against the evils
Of earthly existence
And guarded by none other than yourself
You shall live happily
In this world of change and experience
Samsara.

Bhikku
You are the master
Of your own destiny
You are the master and protector
Of yourself
There is no other
So discipline your mind

The way a merchant
Disciplines his horse
As you steadfastly tread
The Path of Righteousness
Towards the realization
Of the ultimate truth
And you shall be delivered.

In eternal peace and joy
Dwells the bhikku
Who treading the Path of Truth
And abiding by the Dhamma
Has crossed the river of death
And reached
The tranquil shores of Nirvana
Beyond this world of succession and time.

And so the bhikku
Who follows the Dhamma
Though young in years
Shines from afar
With the infinite light of truth
And illumines the world
Like the moon
That emerges
From behind a veil of clouds.

THE BRAHMIN

With courage
And fortitude
Cross the river of passions
Of sorrow and suffering
And strive earnestly
Killing all your selfish desires
As you steadfastly walk upon
The Path of Righteousness
And you shall realize
The deathless reality
Beneath this world
Of duality and separateness.

Cross the river of death
Bravely
Extinguishing the fires of passion
And selfish desires
Still your mind
And as you go beyond
Your likes and dislikes
All the fetters of worldly existence
Shall fall away
As you reach the island of eternal bliss
Nirvana.

He who meditates
Upon his thoughts and feelings
As he walks upon
The Path of Truth
And realizes the ultimate reality
Nirvana
Who is fearless
And beyond
All likes and dislikes
Him I call
A true Brahmin.

Just as the sun
Shines in the daytime
The moon at night
The warrior on the battlefield
And the Brahmin in meditation
So also the Buddha
Shines day and night
Illumining the world
With the eternal light of truth
That shines ever so brightly
From within the very depths
Of his heart and soul.

He who has purged his mind
Of all selfish desires
And evils of earthly existence
Is a true Brahmin.
He who lives peacefully
Whose mind is serene
Is the recluse.
And he who casts out
The impurities from his heart
Is the wanderer.

He who stills his mind
As he walks upon
The Path of Truth
Who is never angry
Whose heart is
Full of compassion
For even those
Who harm him
He is a true Brahmin.

He who has renounced
This world of sensual pleasures
And clings to nothing
Not even himself
Who desists from injuring
And bringing sorrow to others
Sorrow shall not come to him
For he is a true Brahmin.

He who is never harsh
And always kind
In thought, word and deed
Never hurting those around
Who controls
His mind, body and speech
As he mindfully meditates
Upon the Four Noble Truths
Him I call
A true Brahmin.

He who has mastered the Dhamma
The eternal law
Walking in the footsteps of the Buddha
The blessed one
Is worthy of worship
For he is a true Brahmin.

So go forth
And illumine your torch
With the fire of his sacrifice.

Matted hair and deerskin
Prayers and asceticism
And even high birth
Does not make one
Whose mind is full of lust
And selfish desire
A Brahmin
But undying love
For the truth and humanity
And for all creation
Great and small
Makes him
Who believes and practises
The Four Noble Truths
A true Brahmin.

It is not outward show
Of piety and poverty
Saffron robes or lineage
That make him
Whose mind and senses
Remain uncontrolled
A Brahmin
But it is his thoughts
Purged of all evil
Through meditation upon the Four Noble Truths
That make him
A true Brahmin
So, free yourself from selfish desires
And you too shall become a Brahmin.

He who has attained the highest wisdom
And penetrated the Dhamma
The eternal law
Who has lifted the veil of ignorance
And cleansed his thoughts
By breaking through
The chains of selfish desire
Hatred and greed
Who is without doubt and fear
And detached
He is a true Brahmin
For he has realized
The ultimate truth
No impure thought can now pollute him.

He who has woken up
From his sleep
Breaking through
The strap, thong
And chain of karma
That bind him
To the wheel of individuality
And the endless cycle of rebirth
Is awakened
He is a true Brahmin.

He who dwells evermore
In the kingdom of righteousness
Who has realized the ultimate truth
Striving along the Eightfold Path
Who fears nothing
Neither prison nor death
Who though innocent
Endures reproach
With the power of love

No force can defeat
Him I call a true Brahmin.

He whose thoughts
Are always tranquil
Never yielding to anger
Who controls his passions
As he directs the stream of his thoughts
Towards the light of truth
Who is always pure
And self-controlled
Never going astray
From the Path of Righteousness
Him I call a true Brahmin
And this is his last body.

He who has purged his thoughts
Of all selfish desires
And attachments
Lives blissfully
And in freedom
Clinging no more to pleasures
Than a tiny drop of water would
To a lotus leaf
Or the mustard seed
To the tip of a needle
Who has at last gotten rid of
The burden of his karma
Of his past and present existences
Sorrow shall not come near him
For he is a true Brahmin.

He who has
Established himself
In the eternal Dhamma

Walking the Path of Righteousness
Who can discern
The right from the wrong
Who knows all there is to know
Whose wisdom is profound
And understanding deep
Him I call a Brahmin
For he indeed is
Truly enlightened.

He whose wants are few
Who lives in freedom
Totally unbound
By all worldly attachments
To householders and homeless mendicants alike
Delighting in the tranquillity of his thoughts
Him I call a true Brahmin.

He who preaches
And practises loving-kindness
Full of compassion
For all creatures
Great and small
Who has renounced once and for all
Thoughts of violence
And revenge
And put aside
The weapons of war
Who neither kills nor causes to kill
Him I call a true Brahmin.

He who is never hostile
To those who are hostile
Who lives detached
Amongst the selfish

Troubled by thoughts
Of me and mine
Who lives in peace
Amongst those at war
Abiding by the Dhamma
The moral law
Him I call
A true Brahmin.

He who mindfully meditating
Upon the Four Noble Truths
Attains the supreme wisdom
And from whose thoughts
Pride and passion
Hatred and deceit
Fall away
Like the mustard seed
From the point of a needle
Him I call a true Brahmin.

He who is never harsh
Offending no one
Who utters words of wisdom
Easily comprehended by one and all
Who asks not what life can give
But what he can give to life
Him I call a true Brahmin.

He whose mind is free
From all selfish desires
Who dwells evermore in peace and purity
Who craves nothing in this world or the next
As he walks along the Path of Truth
Abiding by the Dhamma
Who is the Lord and master

Of his mind, body and senses
Who has transcended this world
Of succession and time
And gone beyond death
Him I call a true Brahmin.

He who has gone beyond
Good and evil
Who is free from doubt and passions
And has crossed the river of sorrow
Dwells evermore
In unconditioned bliss and purity
Him I call a true Brahmin.

And he indeed is a true Brahmin
Who treading the Path of Truth
Has attained the supreme wisdom
And transcended this world
Of duality and separateness
Liberating himself
From sorrow and sin
And all the evils of worldly existence
As he shines like the full moon
In a cloudless sky.

He who has crossed
The difficult
And turbulent river of death and sorrow
And safely reached the other shore
Where he dwells
In everlasting peace and joy
Him I call a true Brahmin.

He who living in this world
Has renounced everything

His ego and all worldly pleasures
Purging his thoughts
Of feelings of me and mine
Who though homeless
And without possessions
Is ever at home
Wherever he wanders
Who feels ever full
Though he has no ego
Gentle and wise
Him I call a true Brahmin.

He in whom
The desire for existence
And becoming
Has been extinguished
Utterly
Who craves nothing
In this world and beyond
Who has gone beyond sorrow and suffering
Him I call a true Brahmin.

He who has extinguished
Every selfish desire and craving
For all things earthly and celestial
Totally detached from this world
And the heavens above
Who lives in absolute freedom
Wherever he goes
Him I call a true Brahmin.

He who lives unfettered
Totally detached
From humans and nature alike
Who has conquered the world

And himself
Dwells in absolute freedom
Wherever he goes
Him I call a true Brahmin.

He who abiding by the Dhamma
The moral law
Has realized the ultimate truth
Extinguishing his ego
And all thoughts of
"I", "me" and "mine"
Has comprehended the true meaning of life
The arising and dissolution
Of all living things
Knows that nothing is permanent
He is awake
And will never fall asleep again
Him I call a true Brahmin.

He who lives detached and in purity
Is hard to fathom
Without a past or a future
His path to unconditioned freedom
Neither the Gods nor men
Nor the spirits can ever know
He has gone beyond decay and death
And attained the eternal bliss of Nirvana
Noble and wise
Him I call a true Brahmin.

He who possesses and desires
Nothing
Who has renounced all pleasures
And thoughts of personal profit
As he works tirelessly

For the good
Of one and all
That they may live in freedom
Him I call a true Brahmin.

He who is noble and wise
Fearless and awakened
Who has crossed the river of sorrow
And conquered death
Who has realized the ultimate truth
Abiding by the Dhamma
The moral law
And lives in absolute joy and freedom
Him I call a true Brahmin.

He who has reached the end of his journey
Walking the Path of Truth
Who has done
What was to be done
And attained the supreme wisdom
Who has crossed the river of life
Dwells now
In the eternal bliss of Nirvana
Him I call a true Brahmin.

COMMENTARY

THE PAIRS

These pairs of verses are intended to enlighten the minds of not just a learned few, but the entire suffering mass of humanity. Enunciated in these twin verses is first the path of evil, full of sensual pleasure which, though very attractive to human nature, eventually leads to sorrow and suffering in this world and beyond. It is followed by the Path of Righteousness that enjoins the destruction of all worldly desires and attachments in order to attain Nirvana or enlightenment.

In contrast to the evil path that operates on the pleasure principle, the Path of Righteousness lays stress on mental discipline acquired through meditation and by treading the Eightfold Path of Righteousness which, though ridden with thorns, ultimately leads to the cessation of suffering and a release from the cycle of rebirth.

Those who have steadfastly trod the Path of Righteousness, believing in the Four Noble Truths, have attained Nirvana and gained an insight into the reality of this universe. They have realized that the character of this world is determined by our thoughts and our deeds. They believe in the power of the mind that has evolved through innumerable existences in the past. That it is the choice of thought, whether good or evil, that influences human behavior, which in turn has an effect on the society. In reality, it is our thoughts that make this world. We live in a world of thoughts and not of things.

Therefore, to make this world a better place, the Buddha entreated his followers to cultivate positive states of mind by dispelling all evil thoughts. He preached that just as one could be skillful in a particular art or craft, so also one could be skillful in being morally good. By treating others with compassion, one would encourage them to reciprocate these feelings, thereby strengthening the moral fibre of society. This teaching bore a striking similarity to the Christian principle – "Do good unto others that they may do good unto you."

Thus, the Buddha impressed upon his followers that it is the path of evil and the Path of Righteousness that determine the destiny of the individual, the former leading to continual suffering and rebirth and the latter leading to the cessation of suffering, the emancipation from all earthly ties and from the cycle of rebirth.

There is indeed no rebirth for the awakened for they have the power, acquired through meditation and following the Path of Righteousness, of discerning the good from the evil. They are no longer lured by the path of evil with its promise of worldly pleasures having realized that since these pleasures are caused and conditioned, they must end some time, unlike the ineffable bliss of Nirvana that is eternal because it is uncaused and unconditioned.

It is only those who follow the Path of Righteousness, dispelling all egotism, greed, error and hatred from their hearts, who enter the kingdom of righteousness whence there is no return. In the ultimate analysis, it is the moral law that governs the universe and our lives in this world and beyond. Man cannot escape the consequences of his karma or deeds. Just as much as he receives happiness in this life and after by virtue of his good deeds, he suffers the terrible consequences of flouting the Dhamma by virtue of his misdeeds.

There is indeed no greater victory than the victory of truth over falsehood. The paths of evil and righteousness are open to all. It is up to the individual to make his choice between the two destinies. Finally, each person is responsible for his actions. Man is the master of his destiny.

EARNESTNESS

In these verses, the Buddha highlights the importance of earnestly cultivating the habit of mindful meditation whilst seeking the eternal bliss of Nirvana. He warns his followers of the dangers of giving in to slothful ways, as he entreats them to steadfastly tread the Path of Righteousness.

The Buddha who had experimented with the systems of yogic meditation and self-mortification realized their inefficacy in the attainment of the ultimate truth. Although they provided the meditator with long periods of tranquillity and release from their earthly sufferings, these states of mind were only temporary abidings in the here and now, as they were based on the meditator's technical skills at manipulating causes and conditions within himself. They did not lead to the cessation of suffering.

Thus, the Buddha who was convinced that the truth lay within oneself and could not be achieved through any form of external aid in the form of prayers, rituals, self-mortification or even yogic meditation evolved "vipassana", an introspective form of meditation from the yogic absorptions that he had learnt from his teachers Alara Kalama and Udakka Ramaputta.

Vipassana was a mindful and energetic kind of introspective meditation whereby the meditator, by dispassionately analyzing the minutest aspects of his immediate inner and outer states, gradually acquired a moral and intellectual perfection that led to the attainment of Nirvana or enlightenment and gave him an insight into the reality of this universe.

The Buddha further impressed upon his followers the importance of striving ceaselessly along the Path of Truth, in order to attain Nirvana. He entreated them to become more self-possessed and to earnestly cultivate the quality of compassion, as a habit of mind, towards all sentient creation. They were to mindfully reflect on every aspect of their smallest perceptions, feelings and thoughts, so that there would be a dramatic transformation in their emotional and mental make-up, leading to the realization of the ultimate truth.

He further enjoined the practice of mindful meditation in acquiring a mental discipline whereby the meditator would learn to ignore the calls of hunger, physical discomfort and other bodily and mental cravings, as he trained his thoughts towards the realization of the ultimate truth.

According to the Buddha, by simply being mindful and aware whilst treading the Path of Righteousness, objectively analyzing one's immediate thoughts, feelings, perceptions, and ideas, meditating upon their nature, origin and dissolution, one could achieve the moral ideal and a penetrating Buddhist kind of wisdom that would lead to salvation. One could also according to the Buddha, mindfully meditate upon the Four Noble Truths, whilst treading the Path of Righteousness and, on the attainment of the supreme wisdom, be liberated from the cycle of rebirth.

The Buddha believed that those who practised morality and mindful meditation earnestly, as they steadfastly trod the Path of Truth, at times drawing upon their memory in an attempt to understand the reality of this world and their relation to it, had succeeded in creating an island of truth for themselves in this Samsara or ocean of birth and death which no flood could overwhelm.

Through mental discipline and earnestness, they had reached a state of equanimity that transcended pleasure and pain, joy and sorrow, good and evil, in this world itself. By simply being ever-mindful of their physical and mental states, they had experienced the bliss of Nirvana coveted by Gods and men alike. It must be remembered that it was through earnestness that the war-lord Indra, had become the Lord of the Gods of the Vedic pantheon.

Thus, in the words of the Buddha it was "within this fathom long carcass", that the truth about the universe, about the existence, the arising and cessation of suffering lay. The discovery of this truth through the practice of insight meditation and moral conduct whilst earnestly treading the Noble Eightfold Path, eventually led to the emancipation of the individual from the cycle of rebirth.

The Buddha's confidence was based on vipassana or insight meditation which he practised under the peepal or Bodhi tree at Bodhgaya, where at the age of thirty five, in the last watch of the night of the full moon, the ultimate truth was revealed to him.

THE MIND

In Buddhism, unlike the other religious systems of the world, the mind is not considered spirit, consciousness or self as opposed to matter. It is, in fact, considered a sensory organ just like the eyes, ears and the nose. However, the mind belongs to the world of thoughts whereas the other sensory organs belong to the world of visible forms. In reality, all of them belong to this impermanent, ever-changing world of ours.

The mind is not an independent, self-existent entity but is dependent in the conception of ideas and thoughts on its experience of the external world through the sensory organs. Thus, the mind that is constantly conceiving new ideas and thoughts conditioned by feelings and perceptions of the world, is always in a state of flux. Afflicted by worldly feelings of joy and sorrow, love and hatred, doubt and uncertainty, it is unstable and always in a state of activity.

Thus, the Buddha in his prescription for the mental health and equilibrium of an individual, preached the training or disciplining of the mind. This disciplining was essential for progressing in the direction of enlightenment, along the Path of Truth through moral conduct, mindfulness and insight meditation.

The Buddha believed that by mindfully meditating upon one's feelings, thoughts and perceptions, cultivating only those which were essentially good, one could liberate the mind from all negative feelings of anger, hatred and greed, thereby achieving a happier state of existence. He further stressed on the importance of practising meditation for developing a one-pointedness of concentration which he felt, was essential in the attainment of salvation.

The Buddha believed in the power of the mind, which comprising good and evil thoughts, could create and destroy entire civilizations. The mind, he felt, had the capacity to change the course of the history of civilization. He was confident that through the practice of introspective meditation, and by treading the Path of Righteousness, the mind could be controlled and willed to work towards the betterment of mankind.

In the Buddha's philosophy, it was the intention, the choice of thought or mental activity that directed one's thoughts in good, bad or neutral directions that mattered more than the act itself. One acted or behaved through the mind, body or speech, having so willed, in a manner that had a positive or negative impact on oneself and on society. This led the Buddha to regard the intention or choice that preceded one's thoughts and actions as karma.

In fact, the Buddha even regarded an evil thought, although unexpressed in one's outward behaviour as negative karma which he preached would have a bearing on this life and after. Thus, the legal system of the Buddhist order regarded only intentional acts causing harm and injury to others as transgressions. The Buddha believed that by mindfully destroying or simply preventing evil thoughts from arising in the mind and cultivating only those thoughts that are good, one could liberate the mind from all the afflictions of worldly existence and attain enlightenment.

He preached that just as a fletcher straightened his arrows, so also a man could through moral conduct and insight meditation on his immediate physical and mental states discipline his thoughts in accordance with the Dhamma. By blocking out all the distractions of the external world, he could direct his thoughts along the Path of Righteousness, towards the attainment of Nirvana or enlightenment.

The Buddha likened the meditating mind to a fish out of water, breathless and quivering as it struggled for life on the sandy shore. Distracted by worldly desires and attachments, and battling all defilements, such as envy, hatred and greed, the mind that was away from its natural habitat, the truth, was as unhappy and anguished as the fish out of its natural habitat, water.

The Buddha was convinced that by mindfully cultivating a wholesome frame of mind, expunging all negative thoughts and feelings while walking the Path of Truth, one could eventually liberate oneself from the cycle of rebirth and attain enlightenment.

FLOWERS

Just as the garland maker has the power of discerning the most beautiful flowers from the ordinary ones whilst stringing his garland, so also a true follower of the Buddha, on the attainment of enlightenment, through moral conduct and meditation, has the power of discerning the good from the evil in this world of change and experience. It is this power of discernment born out of strenuous effort, whilst treading the Noble Eightfold Path of Righteousness that enables the individual to overcome all evils of the mind, body, and senses, ultimately leading him to the blissful state of Nirvana.

Thus, the Buddha while stressing on the importance of treading the Noble Eightfold Path preached, that through belief and practice of the right kind of speech and action, and earning one's livelihood honourably without resorting to trade in arms and ammunition, illicit liquor or any activity that could create disharmony and disunity amongst people, one can pave one's way to salvation. He further impressed upon his followers the importance of all words and acts of kindness, and adopting a compassionate attitude towards all sentient creation, in order to promote world peace and harmony.

More importantly, while explaining the Eightfold Path, the Buddha laid stress on the individual putting in the right kind of effort in creating a positive state of mind, by consciously destroying all evil thoughts and cultivating only those thoughts that are rooted in the truth. He believed that by being constantly mindful of his immediate mental and bodily states, and the practice of insight meditation upon the minutest aspects of his thoughts, ideas, feelings and perceptions, the individual could achieve a moral and intellectual perfection, that would eventually lead him to the attainment of the supreme wisdom.

This supreme wisdom and its accompanying power of discernment is attained only in the depths of insight meditation, as the meditator mindfully purges his thoughts of all evil while contemplating the Four Noble Truths. It gives him an insight into the reality of this universe. Thus, having established his mind in the truth, treading the Path of Righteousness, the meditator succeeds in restoring his mind to its pristine, original state. He then shines from afar with the intensity of his goodness amongst other mortals.

The meditator makes his life a garland of good deeds that pervades the entire universe with its sweet fragrance, stronger than the fragrance of sandalwood, jasmine, lotus or the tagara flower, as it travels far and wide against the strongest wind.

He is like the lotus flower that grows from the depths of slime, bright and ever-smiling towards the sun. The truthful one remains untouched by all the evils of this world of change and experience. For he has attained the ineffable bliss of Nirvana, that transcends heaven and hell, joy and sorrow; a state that is coveted by the Gods.

Victory then belongs to the enlightened one, for he has by leading a life of virtue and righteousness conquered death and entered the gates of immortality.

THE FOOL

Those who spend their lives in earnest pursuit of sensual pleasures, remain caught in this ocean of birth and death, that is Samsara. They crave for knowledge, existence, wealth, power and other material things in an imperfect, insubstantial and ever-changing world, subjecting themselves to continual suffering in this life and after.

They are fools and immature for they do not realize that what they seek can never bring them everlasting peace and happiness, as it is all a part of this world that is always in a state of flux. Their untrained, unreflecting minds distracted by worldly pleasures, fail to make them understand the importance of moral conduct and meditation in the attainment of the eternal bliss of Nirvana. For it is only in the depths of insight meditation whilst treading the Noble Eightfold Path, that the mind purged of all selfish desires and evil, attains the supreme wisdom and is able to see things as they are.

The enlightened being is then able to perceive things correctly and is no longer misled by sweet utterances, appearances or worldly allurements. Moreover, the attainment of this supreme wisdom is accompanied by a change in quality of both thought and feeling, a kind of self-transformation as well as a self-transcendence. He realizes that the "I", the "self", this individuality of ours to which we are so attached, is in truth, nothing more than a physio-psychological entity, an interdependent, ever-changing, combination of matter, feelings, perceptions, thoughts, ideas and consciousness that falls apart at death.

That death is merely a non-functioning of the physical body, while the desire or will to be or become, to re-exist lives on, and continues to grow, manifesting itself in another form of life after death.

Mature and wise, he knows that all worldly pleasures and attachments belong to this cycle of continuity, Samsara. That the only reality is the ineffable bliss of Nirvana, that can be realized in this life itself, by leading a life of righteousness and the practice of insight meditation.

Indeed, the journey from immaturity to wisdom is long and strenuous, but nevertheless one that leads to the cessation of suffering and a permanent release from the cycle of rebirth. The path to freedom from suffering is open to all, as it holds the hope of enlightenment for even the immature and ignorant through the belief and practice of the Four Noble Truths. Fools then are those who choose the path of falsehood and pleasure. Their thoughts distracted by worldly pleasures, wander aimlessly along the path of evil.

Their untrained, undisciplined minds cannot reflect upon or understand the Four Noble Truths, as revealed by the Buddha. It was, in fact, upon the foundations of the Four Noble Truths that the Buddha built his entire doctrine that showed people the path to the realization of the ultimate reality.

Thus, the Buddha believed that those who spent their lives fulfilling their sensual desires instead of devoting their time to insight meditation whilst treading the Path of Righteousness were subjecting themselves to continual suffering in this life and after. They were fools who by treading the path of falsehood that operated on the pleasure principle, had deluded themselves into believing that what they sought – material well-being and worldly things – would bring them peace and happiness. They did not realize that what they craved for and were attached to, was all a part of a transient and imperfect world that was subject to the natural law of change and was the source of all misery and suffering.

However, the Buddha preached that the fool who realizes his foolishness is wise to the extent that he acknowledges his shortcomings and is willing to tread the Path of Righteousness that will ultimately lead him to enlightenment. He gradually realizes that though his evil and selfish deeds do bring him temporary happiness they eventually bear fruits that are bitter to taste. Knowing that he cannot escape the consequences of his deeds or misdeeds, the fool strives towards the attainment of moral perfection by leading a life of virtue and the practice of insight meditation.

Thus, by realizing the importance of moral conduct and ethical behaviour, the fool acquires some wisdom as he enters the Noble Eightfold Path of Righteousness that ultimately leads him to Nirvana.

THE WISE MAN

The Buddha impressed upon his followers that it was only the right comprehension of the Four Noble Truths that led to the cessation of suffering and a permanent release from the painful cycle of rebirth. This could be acquired through a moral and spiritual perfection reached whilst steadfastly treading the Path of Righteousness.

He preached that a wise man unlike the fool realized the importance of the development of moral character based on the human values of universal love and compassion extended to the entire sentient creation as well as the intellect in the attainment of Nirvana or enlightenment. He believed that wisdom unlike knowledge was uncreated and unoriginated and could be found only in the depths of insight meditation whilst treading the Noble Eightfold Path.

Thus, while explaining the Noble Eightfold Path to his followers, he preached that through moral conduct, the belief and practice of the right kind of speech – abstaining from lying, slander, gossip, abuse and idle talk and the right kind of action – abstaining from murder, theft and adultery and earning one's livelihood honourably, one could pave one's way to Nirvana. More importantly, he said that the individual could by putting in the right kind of effort, in cleansing the mind of all defilements, such as selfish desires, anger, hatred and greed, by consciously destroying and preventing all evil thoughts from arising and cultivating only those that are rooted in the truth, create a positive frame of mind that would eventually lead him to the attainment of the supreme wisdom.

The wise man through ethical behaviour and meditation would then have found the greatest treasure in the form of the Four Noble Truths, the right understanding of which would reveal to him the nature of suffering, how it arises and the way to its cessation. The Buddha was convinced that it was only through an in depth understanding of the nature of suffering that one could trace its origin and find a remedy that could lead to the cessation of suffering.

Thus, in the First Noble Truth the Buddha stated, that suffering was all-pervasive, an inescapable part of human life. Suffering could be defined as the association with all things unpleasant or the separation from all things pleasant.

According to the Second Noble Truth or the Arising of Suffering, the Buddha preached that it was the selfish desire to exist, to be or become that led to continual existence and suffering in the endless cycle of birth and death. This desire sprang from ignorance or delusion that gave one the wrong perception of reality that all worldly pleasures were everlasting.

He assured his followers in the Third Noble Truth about a remedy that would lead to the cessation of suffering and a permanent release from the cycle of rebirth. The Buddha believed that by treading the Noble Eightfold Path of Righteousness or the Fourth Noble Truth, the individual could emancipate himself from all earthly desires and the odious cycle of rebirth and attain Nirvana.

He further impressed upon his followers that the wise man who had realized the ultimate reality by treading the Path of Righteousness, when critical of one's unrighteous ways was actually through his criticism showing the path to salvation. It was therefore better to follow the wise man on the Path of Truth rather than follow the fool on the path of evil and pleasure, for the wise man could reveal hidden treasures in the form of the Four Noble Truths that would lead the individual to the attainment of Nirvana and deliverance from evil.

In the Buddha's philosophy it was not prayers, rituals or self mortification that could lead the individual to enlightenment, but the treading of the Eightfold Path of Righteousness that enjoined the strictest moral discipline, mindfulness and the practice of insight meditation in realization of the ultimate truth.

THE ARHAT

In Buddhism, the Arhat or saint is the fully enlightened being, who through the practice and belief of the Four Noble Truths has released himself from the cycle of birth and death, upon the extinction of the illusion of self. He has reached the end of his spiritual journey, graduating from a Srotapanna, one who has just entered the stream, to becoming a Sakridagamin, one who comes back to this world just once, then to becoming a Anagamin who may be born in the world of Brahma but never returns to this world again and finally to becoming an Arhat on the attainment of the supreme wisdom. He now lives in absolute, unconditioned freedom.

The Buddha rejected the Brahmanic theory of Atman that upheld the belief that the human soul, the atman or self was a part of the Universal Soul, the all-pervasive Brahman or Atman, the ground of all existence. According to this theory, the human soul or self upon deliverance, united with the Universal Soul or Atman when it attained moksha or a permanent release from the cycle of rebirth.

The Buddha preached that the self was in reality nothing more than a worldly physio-psychological entity, an interdependent combination of matter, thoughts, sensations, perceptions and consciousness that was always in a state of flux. Like all compound things, this worldly entity, the self, dissolved upon death.

The self was not, contrary to the popular Brahmanic belief, the "I", the eternal, unchanging soul, the thinker of all thoughts and the doer of all deeds, an independent, immutable entity, a part of the Universal Soul or God, residing in the hearts of men that transmigrated from one birth to another. In the Buddha's philosophy, the soul and mind were not two separate entities but one and the same thing that determined the character of man. In fact, the Buddha believed in the transmigration of character rather than that of the soul.

The Buddha further preached that it was this false idea of self that created selfhood, which in turn gave birth to feelings of envy, hatred and greed. Moreover, like all things caused and conditioned that were subjected to the natural law of change, this worldly self or individuality of ours, was in the Buddha's opinion also an impermanent, ever-changing entity that was a part of the cycle of continuity, or Samsara, conditioned by the karma or deeds of former existences.

He therefore preached that arhatship could only be attained upon the annihilation of the false idea of self, when the mind purged of all egotism, error and greed would be emancipated from the bondage of all worldly desires, upon the realization of the ultimate reality.

The Buddha further regarded the mental volition or desire to exist that caused continual re-existence and suffering in this world also as one's karma, that arose from the belief in the Brahmanic theory of the Atman, the soul, ego or self. He preached that the Arhat did not accumulate karma, since the desire to exist had been utterly extinguished in him.

Thus, he propounded the theory of "Anatta" or "no-self" that denied the existence of the eternal soul or self and laid stress on one's karma or deeds that endured the cycle of rebirth. He impressed upon his followers that man was heir to his karma which determined his destiny in this world and beyond. One's present birth was conditioned by the karma or deeds of former existences, just as much as one's karma or deeds in the present birth would condition one's future state of existence. This was the Law of Karma, the law of cause and effect as stated by the Buddha. According to this law, an individual had to bear the consequences of his deeds and misdeeds of all his previous births – births that could be traced back to the beginning of his consciousness in this cycle of continuity.

However, the Buddha preached that even the evil-doer could by treading the Path of Righteousness, by gradually and mindfully dispelling all feelings of egotism, hatred and greed from his mind attain arhatship. Noble and wise, the Arhat represented the ideal Buddhist character. Patient like the earth and firm like the threshold, he was pure like the lake without mud, reflecting the infinite light of truth.

Just as the flight of birds is trackless, so also the path to arhatship and unconditioned freedom is trackless, without any karmic residue. By destroying every selfish desire for sensual pleasure and existence, through the practice of morality and meditation, the Arhat attains the supreme wisdom that enables him to see things as they are, without name or label. Thus, the Arhat having attained nobility of thought, word and deed emancipates himself from the fetters of selfhood and worldly desires, and dwells peacefully in the unconditioned freedom of Nirvana.

THE THOUSANDS

Those who have the right perception of the Dhamma are the truly enlightened beings. They have through the belief and practice of the Four Noble Truths attained the supreme wisdom that has given them a penetrating insight into the Dhamma, and they are able to see things as they are.

Dhamma is the truth, the law of righteousness that governs the entire universe. It encompasses all things caused and conditioned that are a part of Samsara, this impermanent world of change and experience, as well as those things related to the uncaused and unconditioned state of Nirvana.

Thus, the Four Noble Truths that are revealed to the individual during deep meditation when the mind purged of all defilements becomes the habitation of the truth, give him the right comprehension of the Dhamma. He then learns that all worldly things, in their native state, are nothing but the truth. The truth can only be realized by cultivating thoughts that are essentially good and by consciously destroying and preventing evil or bad thoughts from arising in the mind.

Moreover, the individual also realizes that the false idea of self, the "I", this individuality of ours to which we cling so passionately, creates feelings of "me'" and "mine", which in turn give rise to selfhood and thirst that lead to renewed existence, in this ocean of birth and death, Samsara. In truth, this self is an interdependent combination of matter, sensations, perceptions, thoughts and consciousness, which like all compound things in nature, has within itself, the seed of dissolution. Thus, this worldly self like all things caused and conditioned is imperfect and impermanent, and dissolves upon death.

Death is in reality, only a link in the chain of existence of an individual, of cause and effect, of a series of births and deaths that can be traced to the beginning of his consciousness caused by ignorance. The Buddha believed that the main cause of the cycle of rebirth was ignorance. This was the root cause of all evil. It caused and conditioned volitional actions which in turn conditioned consciousness. This consciousness conditioned mental and physical phenomena that conditioned the five sense organs and the mind. These sense organs and the mind conditioned contact and through contact was conditioned sensation. Sensation conditioned desire or thirst which conditioned clinging. This clinging conditioned the process of becoming which conditioned birth. Birth in turn conditioned pain, death, sorrow and lamentation, in this endless cycle of continuity.

Thus, according to the Buddha, the false idea of self created selfhood and conditioned the desire or thirst for re-existence, causing rebirth in the cycle of continuity, Samsara. He impressed upon his followers that the individual by dispelling ignorance through the right understanding of the Four Noble Truths, realizing the impermanent nature of the worldly self, liberated himself from the cycle of birth and death.

He stressed that it is only one's karma that endures the cycle of rebirth and decides one's fate in this world and beyond. According to the Law of Karma, the law of cause and effect, good deeds lead to better rebirth and ultimately salvation while bad deeds lead to continual suffering and rebirth, in this world of name and form.

There is, however, no immutable or eternal human soul, which is a part of the Universal Soul or God that transmigrates from one birth to another. The theory of soul, the atman, the ego or self is merely an illusion evolved for man's need for self-protection and self-preservation. It is only our thoughts, desires, the will to re-exist, to become, to continue that takes another form of life after death, causing continual rebirth in this world.

Thus, the Buddha emphasised the importance of the attainment of the supreme wisdom, upon the destruction of the illusion of self, when thinking stops and thoughts purged of all evil stilled, in giving one an insight into reality. He further impressed upon his followers the inefficacy of prayers, rituals and self-mortification and all forms of external aid in the attainment of salvation. According to him, the truth lay within oneself, and could only be realized through the complete expunging of worldly desires when the mind freed from the fetters of ignorance and delusion and purged of all evil was restored to its native state, the truth.

He therefore explained that a word of Dhamma, rooted in the truth, uttered by the wise man brought greater peace of mind to an individual than a poem of a thousand beautiful and meaningless verses or a speech of a thousand senseless words. He believed that the conquest of the self through mental discipline and moral conduct was greater than a thousand victories on the battlefield. The conquest of the self led to liberation from the cycle of rebirth and the eternal bliss of Nirvana, whilst victory in war though it brought fame and glory to the victor kept him in bondage to worldly desires. Moreover, according to the Buddha, the victory over the self was one which even the mightiest of Gods could not turn into defeat.

In the Buddha's philosophy, the wise man who had attained the unconditioned bliss of Nirvana was to be revered and paid homage to, for he could by imparting his wisdom, show people the Path of Truth that would ultimately lead them to salvation.

EVIL

The Buddha did not believe in God or any supernatural power, but the Law of Karma, the law of cause and effect that governs all mental and physical events in the lives of men. In his philosophy, there is no God or any supernatural power sitting on moral judgement on the deeds of men. It is the Law of Karma that, according to their deeds and misdeeds, decides their fate in this world and the next.

Karma is not a reward or effect, as is commonly understood by most people, but is an action or deed that produces positive or negative results in the cycle of rebirth. Thus, good karma leads to happiness and a better rebirth while bad karma leads to suffering and continual existences in the endless cycle of rebirths. One inherits the karmas of previous existences, which determine the course of one's life in this world of change and experience.

The Buddha regarded volition, the intention, or choice that precedes speech and action as an individual's karma that leads an individual to behave in a particular way through his mind, body and speech. Thus, in his opinion, it was only intentional or volitional acts that had karmic effects causing becoming and continual re-existence in the cycle of birth and death. In fact, the Buddha regarded all impulses, actions and reactions as the outcome of the mental choice or intention of an individual.

He believed that all unconscious impulses that were generally regarded as automatic responses to a stimulus, were actually the result of habitual conscious choices that were conditioned by ignorance about the true nature of things. These impulses, the last thoughts of a dying man survived his death, entering a new form of life, and determined its character. Thus, good impulses endowed the new physio-psychological entity with physical well- being and a pleasant disposition whilst bad impulses deprived the physio-psychological entity of physical well being and a pleasant disposition. It was therefore volition or choice that made an individual's character and his world, for having so chosen an individual spoke and acted in a manner that had karmic effects, in this cycle of continuity, Samsara.

Thus, volition or mental choice had great power conditioned by ignorance or delusion about the nature of reality that all worldly pleasures are everlasting that created the insatiable thirst for existence in an impermanent world. It was this thirst bound by ignorance, the source of all evil, that created attachment to the self and selfhood, which in turn gave birth to feelings of egotism, hatred and greed, subjecting the individual to continual suffering in this caused and conditioned world of ours.

True bliss then lay in the attainment of the ineffable state of Nirvana that transcended joy and sorrow, life and death. Nirvana delivered the individual from evil upon the extinction of the illusion of self. The state of enlightenment or Nirvana as preached by the Buddha could only be attained by strictly adhering to his moral code that enjoined his followers to purge their minds, bodies and speech of all evil that was obstructing their path to salvation.

Thus, the Buddha classified lying, slander, gossip and idle talk as evils of the speech; adultery, cheating, killing, and theft as evils of the body; and envy, greed, hatred and error as evils of the mind. He believed that by avoiding these ten evils, the evil-doer could through the practice of mindful meditation, expiate all his sins in this life itself and attain the eternal bliss of Nirvana.

More importantly, the evil-doer through ethical behaviour and insight meditation upon his impulses, feelings and perceptions, by breaking through every habitual way of thinking that produces karmic results repeatedly, would cleanse his thoughts of all defilements and desires, making himself the embodiment of the truth.

PUNISHMENT

Buddhism recognizes only volitional action as an individual's karma. According to the intention of the doer, these actions produce good or bad effects, known as karma-phala or the fruits of karma. Thus, all volitional acts that are good lead to better rebirth, health and fortune, while all volitional acts that are bad lead to rebirth in a lower grade of existence, insanity, infirmity and a loss of fortune. This is the Law of Karma, the law of cause and effect that operates on the principle "as you sow, so shall you reap."

The individual inherits the karmas of former existences that can be traced back to the dawn of the evolution of his consciousness, to beginningless time. He is, in fact, the product of the karmas of all his past births, a series of causes and effects, which shape his character. Thus, the experiences of his present life are the results of his deeds or misdeeds of countless past existences, some of which have taken several rebirths to bear fruit. The individual simply cannot escape the consequences of his karma.

In Buddhism, there is no eternal soul or self, but an individual's karma that survives the cycle of rebirth and conditions the course of his life in this world and beyond. According to the Buddha, it was volition, choice or the selfish thirst for sensual pleasures and existence that caused re-becoming and re-existence in this cycle of continuity, Samsara. However, an individual could by killing this selfish thirst through the practice of morality and meditation, escape the pain of continual existence and attain the supreme wisdom. For this wisdom would give him the right perception of reality about the transient nature of all forms of worldly existence.

According to the Buddha's doctrine, this supreme wisdom was not knowledge based on data of the created world, but the truth that lay within oneself, discovered through the attainment of a moral, spiritual and intellectual perfection in deep insight meditation. The Buddha believed that through ethical behaviour and meditation, this continual re-existence, the constant formation of a new physio-psychological entity in the cycle of rebirth could cease upon the discovery of the truth.

In the Buddha's philosophy, ethical behaviour meant abstinence from evils of the mind, body and speech through the conscious cultivation of noble qualities such as love, kindness, tolerance, charity and compassion, in accordance with the Dhamma. This would benefit not only the individual but society as well. In fact, it was compassion and his boundless love for humankind that were the chief motivating factors in the Buddha preaching his doctrine, after the awakening, to an ignorant world.

Thus, the Buddha exhorted his followers to purify their minds by skillfully cultivating only those thoughts that are rooted in the truth and dispelling or preventing evil thoughts from arising. His moral code evolved for the spiritual uplift of the individual also aimed at the promotion of peace and harmony in the world. The Buddha did not view the individual in isolation but as a member of society, and worked tirelessly, out of his compassion for mankind, towards the welfare of society.

He warned his followers, that wherever they went, whether to the mountains, to distant lands or the high seas, they simply could not escape the ill effects of their bad karma. He further impressed upon them that those who sought happiness by injuring others, especially the innocent, would sooner or later suffer the grievous consequences of their evil deeds. They only way to happiness, was by walking the Path of Truth.

The Buddha further preached that the individual, by exercising mindfulness upon all activities of the mind and body, meditating dispassionately on all his thoughts and feelings, could succeed in purging the mind of all defilements that would lead him to the realization of the ultimate truth.

Thus, having killed every selfish desire, there would be no karmic residue for the enlightened being. His thoughts pure and sublime, stilled upon the attainment of Nirvana, would have released him from the painful cycle of birth and death.

OLD AGE

According to the Buddha, birth that creates individuality and separateness is attended by the inevitable pain and suffering of disease, decay, old age, and finally death. The birth of an individual is only a link in a series of causes and effects of innumerable grades of existences that can be traced back to beginning of time, in this cycle of continuity.

The Buddha viewed the event of the birth of an individual with a sense of detachment. He believed that it subjected him to the inevitable suffering of worldly existence. In his philosophy, an individual was in reality nothing more than an interdependent combination of five aggregates of attachment namely 1. Aggregate of Matter – that included the Four Great Elements of solidity, fluidity, heat and motion as well as the Derivatives – that included the five sensory organs and their corresponding external objects as well as thoughts and ideas, 2. Aggregate of Sensations, 3. Aggregate of Perceptions, 4. Aggregate of Mental Formations which encompassed all volitional actions and lastly 5. Aggregate of Consciousness, that were always in a state of flux. The individual, like all compound things in nature had within himself the germs of arising, decay, and dissolution and was subject to the natural law of change. The Buddha preached that since none of these five aggregates was the same for two consecutive moments, with each state of existence conditioning the next, it was better to seek that which was permanent, the eternal bliss of Nirvana.

He likened the stream of life of an individual to an ever-flowing mountain river in this cycle of continuity, Samsara, and urged his followers to find a way to end the sorrow and pain of continual existence through the belief and practice of the Four Noble Truths. This would ultimately lead them to salvation. Neither a pessimist nor an optimist, the Buddha was, above all, a realist who viewed life with all its trials and tribulations, joys and sorrows, with the detachment and objectivity of a renouncer.

In fact, long ago, the four visions of an old man, a diseased man, a corpse, and an ascetic that the Buddha had encountered before his enlightenment in his youth, on his first journey into the streets of Kapilavasthu had revealed to him the impermanence of human life. These visions made him realize the inevitability of old age, disease, decay and death in the life of an individual. He therefore regarded the striving towards the preservation of beauty and youth as futile. He further preached that the individual upon the attainment of enlightenment, would learn to look upon beauty and youth dispassionately, realizing that with the onset of old age his mental faculties would weaken and he would gradually lose his beauty and physical strength. Indeed, the Buddha over the ages has proven correct, since no amount of scientific invention or medical advancement has yet been able to overcome old age and death.

So, the Buddha entreated his followers to strive for the uncaused and unconditioned bliss of Nirvana, by treading the Path of Truth, expunging all desires for material wealth, position, power, knowledge and existence and making their minds the abode of the truth. He also impressed upon them in some of these verses the importance of acquiring spiritual discipline in youth instead of expending all their energies in pursuit of sensual pleasures, in order to come to terms with reality in old age.

He likened the house builder to an individual's thirst or selfish craving for repeated existence. This he regarded as the main cause for continual birth and death in this world of experience and change. He believed that the individual on the attainment of enlightenment would have realized that it is this selfish desire to be, to become other than what one is, to exist, that leads to endless rebirths in a transient world, subjecting him continually to the pain of disease, decay, old age, and death. He would also learn that old age and death can only be conquered through the practice of morality and meditation whilst treading the Noble Eightfold Path of Righteousness that will ultimately lead him to the unageing, deathless and blissful state of Nirvana.

THE SELF

A revolutionary, the Buddha challenged the Brahmanic theory of the Atman, the Soul or Self, upheld by the most renowned sages of that time. According to this theory, the human soul, the ego or self was a part of the eternal or Universal Soul, the imperishable Atman, Brahman or God, from whom all creation emanated. The self or soul of man was thus considered an independent, indestructible, unchanging entity that survived the endless cycle of birth and death.

The soul as preached by the Brahmin sages was the "I", the doer of all deeds and the thinker of thoughts, which through the various practices of extreme asceticism, that purged it of all its impurities or the practice of yogic meditation eventually attained moksha or a permanent release from the cycle of rebirth, uniting with the all-pervasive Brahman or Atman.

The Buddha regarded the belief in the eternity of the self or soul as the gravest error made by humankind, for it created selfhood, which in turn gave rise to feelings of envy, egotism, pride, hatred and greed, subjecting the individual to continual existence in this cycle of individuality. He preached that enlightenment or Nirvana could only be attained, upon the complete annihilation of the illusion of self.

The Buddha further believed that the error in the Atman theory lay in the scant attention it paid to the building or reshaping of human character, in accordance with the Dhamma, in delivering the individual from evil. He preached that no amount of prayers, sacrifice or self-mortification could release the individual from the pain of continual existence while he remained evil in both thought and in deed. In his philosophy, the ideas of morality and self-liberation were inextricably linked.

Thus, the Buddha propounded the theory of "Anatta", no-soul or no-self, that denied the existence of the eternal soul or God, throwing man upon his own resources in the realization of the ultimate truth. Indeed, the theory of Anatta was the light of wisdom that illumined the minds of the Buddha's followers, giving them an insight into the reality of this world.

According to the Anatta theory, the self or the "I" was not a part of the Universal Soul or God but simply a worldly entity, composed of the five, interdependent physical and mental aggregates. This worldly entity, the self or individual, like all compound things in nature, was under the law of cause and effect, an ever-changing, impermanent entity that had within itself the germs of arising, decay and dissolution. There was no immortal soul or self within or outside these five aggregates, in the universe or anywhere outside of it. Therefore, the Buddha regarded attachment to the worldly self, this individuality of ours, conditioned by ignorance, as the cause of all suffering, as it led to constant re-existence and becoming in this caused and conditioned world.

He preached to his followers, that in the worldly context, for the sake of identification it was better to consider the body that fell into the aggregate of matter, as the "I", since it did not change with the same rapidity as the other aggregates did, and was relatively more stable. The Buddha who upon the attainment of enlightenment or Nirvana had gained a penetrating insight into reality, preached the existence of the self as a conventional truth in the worldly sense as is commonly understood by people, impressing upon his followers that the ultimate truth was that in reality there was indeed no self.

The Buddha further regarded the self , the "I" or being, as a product of all his good and bad karmas, of innumerable past existences, that can be traced back to the beginning of his consciousness. He denied the existence of an immortal atman or soul and entreated his followers to work out their own salvation with diligence. In fact, when he said "Self is the lord of self", he stressed on human endeavour in working strenuously towards the realization of the ultimate truth. He urged his followers to rely only on themselves and the Dhamma in the attainment of Nirvana.

Thus, the Buddha repeatedly impressed upon his followers that an individual lived through the karmas of his present as well as all his past existences in this world. The only way he could liberate himself from this cycle of rebirth was through moral conduct and meditation, that would lead him to the blissful state of Nirvana, upon the extinction of the illusion of the self.

THE WORLD

The Buddha looked upon the world, a part of this cycle of continuity, conditioned by ignorance, as nothing more than an illusion. He compared this world to a mirage, an empty bubble that no sooner was it formed than it burst into the deep, immeasurable ocean. There was indeed nothing permanent or stable in this world, with each moment of existence conditioning the next, that could bring the individual lasting peace and happiness. He therefore described the nature of this world and all forms of worldly existence as dukkha, a word which in ordinary usage means suffering.

In his philosophy, there existed a world of visible forms experienced through the body, the eyes, the nose, ears, and the tongue as well as a world of thoughts experienced by the mind. The worlds of visible form and thoughts were interdependent and together they constituted the world of the individual. Since neither the world of visible forms nor the world of thoughts were stable for two consecutive moments, the Buddha regarded attachment to all forms of worldly existence as the source of misery and suffering. Indeed one realizes while deep in insight meditation that no sooner does a particular thought arise in the mind, than it is replaced by another, and so the stream of thought continues flowing in this fashion, into this ocean of birth and death, Samsara.

According to the Buddha, this world of ours was characterized by duality, combination, separation and change. He believed that some of the happiest moments of an individual's existence in it were marked by varying degrees of pain. Therefore, he preached complete detachment from one's near and dear ones, from one's physical state as well as mental states of peace, tranquillity, and joy as they were all very transient in nature.

The Buddha impressed upon his followers that hidden in this world of change and experience, was the underlying, unchanging, ultimate reality in which there was no duality, combination or separation. Independent of all causes and conditions it was the truth that was found and not created, upon the extinction of the illusion of self, by treading the Noble Eightfold Path of Righteousness.

Furthermore, according to the Buddha, the truth was all-pervasive and could even be found in stones and trees although they lacked consciousness as well as in animals and humans who possessed a consciousness of the self. In fact, it was the consciousness of this self, that was in reality, no more than an ever-changing worldly entity composed of the five mental and physical aggregates , that created selfhood from which flowed all the evils of worldly existence that subjected the individual to continual rebirth in this world of pain and suffering.

In the Buddha's philosophy, it was the mental volition, the will or selfish thirst to exist, to be or become other than what one is, to grow, to re-exist in another state, which was a great force that directed lives and in fact the whole world forward, in good, bad or neutral directions. This force determined the character of individuals and this world. Thus, mental volition that could be equated with intention or choice made under the delusion that the world held lasting pleasures led to the pain and suffering of re-existence and becoming in this cycle of continuity.

True bliss then lay in treading the Noble Eightfold Path that would ultimately lead to the cessation of suffering upon the realization of the ultimate truth.

THE BUDDHA

The attainment of Buddhahood or enlightenment is the outcome of a moral and intellectual perfection achieved not in a single lifetime, but through innumerable births in the past, starting from the beginning of consciousness of the individual. It is the result of enduring patiently the pain and suffering of countless births and deaths without ever deviating from the Path of Truth, howsoever great the cause.

In the Buddha's philosophy, to evolve through the lower grades of existence, from a tree to an animal and then to a human being was a blessing, as he believed that it was only the human being with his highly developed mental and physical faculties who was capable of attaining Buddhahood or enlightenment. The Buddha preached that even in his lifetime, an individual could, through the belief and practice of the Four Noble Truths become a Buddha, upon the attainment of the supreme wisdom that would give him an insight into reality.

He explained to his followers, that through moral conduct and the practice of insight meditation, the individual could realize the absolute truth, the Dhamma that would give him the right perception of reality. He would then become aware that all forms of worldly existence were subject to the natural law of change and could never bring him everlasting peace and happiness. Therefore, the Buddha entreated his disciples to be self-reliant. He advised them not to seek happiness in this transient world, but to seek it through the realization of the truth that lay within themselves. This could only be done by striving earnestly along the Path of Righteousness that led to salvation.

He further preached, that by simply taking refuge in the Buddha, the Dhamma or his doctrine and the Sangha, the Buddhist order of monks, the disciple would be shown the Noble Path that would ultimately lead to the cessation of suffering.

It must be borne in mind, that the Dhamma was immensely wide in its scope, encompassing all things conditioned and unconditioned, caused and uncaused within and outside this universe. It was the all-pervasive truth without a Self, Atman or God and the basis of all creation. The Dhamma was the moral law that governed the entire universe.

According to the Buddha, any individual could attain enlightenment or Buddhahood by treading the Eightfold Path of Righteousness. Moreover, by earnestly reshaping his character, in accordance with the Dhamma, he would ultimately be liberated from the fetters of selfhood that subjected him to the pain and suffering of repeated existence in this cycle of rebirth.

This could be achieved by the complete destruction of all selfish desires and by consciously cultivating noble thoughts of love, patience, kindness, sympathy and tolerance, as a habit of mind. The Buddha believed that it was selfish desires and other defilements such as anger, lust, hatred and envy which if not extinguished in the mind, clung to it through several births, dimming the vision of the ultimate truth. It was only a pure mind, purged of all evil that could attain the highest wisdom that would enable the individual to see the truth.

The enlightened being would then become aware that in reality there was no such thing as an eternal soul, the atman or self that dwelt in the hearts of men and that the only thing that endured was his karma, the sum of his good and evil deeds, through the endless cycle of rebirth. That the false idea of self was just a mental projection, nothing more than an illusion. It was the source of all evil for it created selfishness and feelings of "me" and "mine" which in turn gave rise to egotism, ill will and greed.

Thus, by establishing the truth in his mind, through the belief and practice of the Four Noble Truths, the individual would have liberated himself from the bonds of worldly existence and attained Buddhahood.

HAPPINESS

Happiness is a state of mind, caused and conditioned by an individual's positive experiences in this world of change and experience, Samsara. Since this worldly happiness is not independent of causes and conditions, it can never be permanent, sooner or later giving way to feelings of unhappiness, dissatisfaction and frustration in an imperfect, ever-changing world. Happiness then as a state of mind is impermanent and whatever is impermanent in nature is the source of dukkha or suffering.

Dukkha as enunciated by the Buddha in the First Noble Truth or the Truth of Suffering is "the union with all things unpleasant, the separation from all things pleasant, or simply the inability to achieve what one desires." The Buddha described life accompanied by the inevitable pain of birth, separation, disease, decay, lamentation, old age and death as dukkha. He preached that by understanding the all-pervasive nature of suffering in human life, an individual could trace its origin and thereby find a remedy that would lead to the cessation of suffering.

The Buddha believed that the enduring happiness of Nirvana was not an illusion but a reality hidden in this world that could be attained through moral conduct, mental discipline and the attainment of wisdom, in this life itself. It is, however, noteworthy, that although the moral code the Buddha evolved enjoined the strictest moral discipline from the monks in the observance of absolute chastity and complete renunciation, it was adaptable to the realities of the laity who had to live in this world and bear children while performing their household duties.

Moreover, the Buddha who was a pragmatist realized the importance of economic prosperity in the promotion of peace and harmony in this world. He believed that economic hardship led to immoral behaviour, which in turn caused strife and unhappiness in society. While he never despised wealth, he warned his followers about the dangers of being unduly attached to it. Wealth, like all worldly things, was impermanent and could never bring everlasting peace and happiness to the individual. For, the happiness experienced through the accumulation of wealth could lead to the employment of dishonourable means in earning one's livelihood, such as trading in arms and ammunition, drugs, illicit liquor and other immoral activities. These in turn could lead to the disintegration of society. In his philosophy, the evil of seeking happiness by harming others would eventually recoil on the evil-doer in this life and after.

Thus, in order to promote a happier state of existence in this world, the Buddha enjoined his followers to abstain from all evils of the mind, body and speech as they walked along the Path of Righteousness. He believed that the individual by bringing happiness to others by abstaining from these evils would encourage them to behave in a similar manner, thereby strengthening the moral fibre of the society.

The Buddha further impressed upon his followers, that abiding happiness could only be attained through mental discipline acquired through the practice of insight meditation or vipassana, whereby the individual by mindfully and dispassionately analyzing the minutest aspects of his mental and bodily states, could achieve a moral and spiritual perfection, that would lead to the attainment of the supreme wisdom. The individual would then be able to see things as they are and free himself from all worldly desires, upon the realization that there is indeed no abiding happiness in this caused and conditioned world. The enlightened being would then live in a state of absolute bliss and unconditioned freedom untouched by all the joys and sorrows of worldly existence.

PLEASURE

It is thirst, an insatiable craving for sensual pleasures, re-existence and re-becoming that leads to repeated births, in this cycle of continuity, Samsara. It must be borne in mind, however, that Buddhism recognizes no "being" within or outside this universe but recognizes the individual as a product of a series of causes and effects. He is always in the process of "becoming" other than what he is, and the thirst to constantly re-exist in some other state, is what leads to rebirth in this world. Since all forms of earthly existence are conditioned, relative, interdependent and always in a state of flux, there is nothing permanent in this world that is independent of causes and effects, that can bring abiding joy to the individual.

Even feelings that are perceived as pleasure in the mind through certain pleasant and satisfying experiences of the sensory organs with the external world are, sooner or later, replaced by unpleasant or painful feelings caused and conditioned by situations and experiences that are at times beyond the control of the individual. Moreover, since all feelings of pleasure are impermanent in nature, based on the experiences of the external, ever-changing world, they are a source of suffering.

The feeling of pleasure arises whenever there is a visible object, sound, smell or anything in the world that is appealing to the senses. It is human nature to constantly crave for sensual pleasures that creates attachment to this transient world of name and form, thereby subjecting the individual to the suffering of repeated births in this cycle of continuity. However, this thirst for pleasure is very wide in its scope, and it also encompasses the pleasure that one derives in holding onto ideals, thoughts and beliefs or simply being in the "know" of things. Thus, it is this thirst or craving for sensual pleasures and existence that leads to feelings of pain and suffering when the objects of pleasure no longer exist or simply change into objects of displeasure.

Since each state of existence is never the same for two consecutive moments, to constantly seek everlasting pleasure is to subject oneself to misery and suffering in this world of change and experience. True bliss then lies in transcending all fleeting feelings of pleasure and pain, joy and sorrow, by realizing that which is permanent, the ultimate truth or Nirvana that lies hidden in this imperfect and transient world.

Thus, the Buddha preached that through the belief and practice of the Four Noble Truths the individual could attain enlightenment or Nirvana, upon the extinction of the illusion of self. For he would then realize that this "self" of ours which we perceive as a self-existent, immutable and eternal entity, the "I" , the doer of all deeds or karma, is in truth, an organism composed of mental and physical aggregates that are constantly changing. That the self is not immortal or a part of the all-pervasive Brahman or Atman, but merely a worldly entity, which like all compound things in nature dissolves upon death.

The Buddha further preached that the constant craving for pleasure arose from ignorance – from the false idea about the eternity of the self, the "I", or the soul. The feeling of pleasure, a part of the five aggregates that constituted the worldly self was impermanent and therefore a source of pain and suffering.

According to the Buddha, the thirst for sensual pleasure and existence was a great force that survived the death of an individual and impeded his progress along the path to enlightenment. He believed that it was only upon the extinction of this thirst for sensual pleasure and existence that an individual could attain the eternal bliss of Nirvana and thus be released from the cycle of rebirth.

ANGER

The Buddha viewed anger as one of the five hindrances – the others being lust, languor, worry and doubt – in the attainment of Nirvana or enlightenment. He believed that anger destabilized the mind, causing irrationality and led the thoughts astray from the Path of Truth onto the path of evil and falsehood. The vision of the mind overpowered with angry thoughts got blurred. Therefore an angry mind was unable to clearly see or discern the truth, as one struggled against the forces of evil whilst treading the Noble Eightfold Path of Righteousness.

Anger that drove an individual to resort to violence, the use of hurtful and abusive language, and other forms of undesirable behaviour, had bad karmic effects. The individual through his irrational, uncontrolled thoughts and bad behaviour inflicted pain and suffering on others, thereby causing them to behave in a similar manner with him. Eventually, he had to suffer the consequences of his evil deeds born out of anger, an emotion, which according to the Buddha, though it brought temporary relief to the individual when it was released, inevitably led to suffering in this world and beyond.

The Buddha preached that by overcoming anger with non-anger, by skillfully cultivating good and gentle thoughts, as a habit of mind, one could achieve a tranquil and joyful state of mind that would be conducive to rationality and the realization of the ultimate truth.

He impressed upon his followers that the individual by mindfully meditating upon his inner and outer states, his nature, the arising, and cessation of all his feelings, thoughts and perceptions, would be able to understand the nature of his negative emotion, anger, trace its origin and find a way that would lead to the cessation of anger and all the evils that emanate from it.

According to the Buddha, it was the unfulfilled selfish desire for sensual pleasure, for existence and the non-existence of all unpleasant mental and physical states that gave rise to anger. It was human nature to desire anything pleasant or attractive, and when this desire was not fulfilled, it created feelings of anger, ill-will and hatred in the mind of the individual. This desire conditioned by the delusion about the immortality of the soul or ego and the feeling that there were some lasting pleasures in this world, gave birth to feelings of anger and ill will, when an individual was frustrated in his efforts of achieving mental or physical happiness in life. Since, nothing in this world was permanent, with each moment of existence conditioning the next, to seek lasting satisfactions in it only caused him pain.

Thus, the Buddha impressed upon his followers that it was only by mindfully meditating on the nature of all their selfish desires and attachments, how they arise and pass away, that they could extinguish them completely, and thereby deliver themselves from the evils of anger, hatred and greed.

IMPURITY

It is ignorance about the nature of reality that creates the thirst for seeking the intransient in a transient world, which in turn causes attachment to all things worldly, subjecting the individual to the pain of repeated existence in this endless cycle of rebirth. The Buddha, traced all the impurities of the mind to ignorance, the false idea of self, which he felt created feelings of "me" and "mine", giving birth to selfishness and thirst, a powerful force that survived the death of the individual, manifesting itself in a new form of life in the cycle of continuity.

The Buddha regarded the Brahmanic belief in the human soul or self being a part of the immortal Atman or Brahman, as no more than a mental projection developed to satisfy man's selfish desire to continue in some other state of existence. He therefore exhorted his followers not to go by hearsay and blindly believe in religious theories, no matter how evolved they were, out of tradition or respect for authority but to base their beliefs upon the provable truth, upon what they could experience and observe "here and now". In fact, he even went to the length of telling his disciples that they were not obliged to follow his teachings. For he firmly believed, that their faith in his doctrine had to be based on their personal experience and the conviction that it would show them the way to salvation.

He preached that as long as one remained in bondage to the false idea of self, one would continue to be afflicted by feelings of lust, hatred, pride, conceit and greed in this life and after. These impurities, according to the Buddha, did not die with the death of the individual but lived on clinging like dirt to his thoughts as he entered a new form of life. Like iron that is corroded by the rust it breeds, these self-created impurities ate into his good karma or deeds that he had accumulated over several births.

Gradually, with the passage of time, these impurities festered and dominated an individual's thoughts, clouding his judgement about the reality of this world. Unchecked and uncontrolled, they became a part of his personality, as they led him on the path of evil and falsehood – towards destruction.

However, the Buddha preached that the individual by exercising self-control in abstaining from the evils of the body, tongue and mind could negate his bad karma or deeds that would lead to happiness in this life and after. By not resorting to theft or murder, howsoever great the cause and not committing adultery, he could build a peaceful environment not only for others but for himself as well. Furthermore, by abstaining from lying, slander, abuse and gossip, speaking only the truth from the goodness of his heart, he would encourage others to speak kindly to him, thereby creating an atmosphere of goodwill.

More importantly, the Buddha preached that by meditatively cultivating an attitude of loving-kindness towards all sentient beings, an individual could create the right frame of mind, joyful and compassionate, that would ultimately enable him to see reality. Thus, by mindfully overcoming the five hindrances to salvation, namely lust, anger, worry, languor and doubt, through the practice of morality and meditation, whilst treading the Path of Righteousness, he could gradually purify his mind and attain Nirvana.

THE PERSON ESTABLISHED IN THE DHAMMA

In Buddhist philosophy, the Dhamma is the moral law that governs the entire universe, prescribing the course of movement of the planets and stars right down to the smallest form of life on earth. The timeless Dhamma denotes not only the laws of nature but also traditions, customs and the laws of the castes and living in accordance with it, is the way to perfect happiness. It is the limitless whole underlying this world of duality and separateness, the basis of all existence and creation.

The Dhamma is the hidden truth, the intransient in this transient world of name and form, present in all forms of creation right from stones and trees that lack consciousness to animals and humans who have a very developed sense of self. There is indeed no term in Buddhism that is wider in its scope than the Dhamma, for it encompasses not only that which is caused and conditioned but also the uncaused and unconditioned state of Nirvana. The Dhamma is the eternal truth, and those who establish themselves firmly in it, through moral conduct and the practice of mindful meditation, attain the unconditioned bliss and freedom of Nirvana. Through ethical striving whilst treading the Path of Righteousness, they gain a penetrating insight into the Dhamma, and are able to see things as they are, upon the attainment of the supreme wisdom.

The Dhamma is without a self, either within or anywhere outside the individual. For the Buddha believed that is was the false idea of the self, caused by ignorance, from which all the evils of worldly existence emanated. According to the Buddha, most of the errors of human judgement arose from the Brahmanic theory of Atman, the immortal soul or self of man, believed to be a part of the Universal Soul or God that transmigrated from one birth to another.

The Buddha felt that since the soul or self of man, the ego, the "I", the actor behind all actions, was perceived as no different from the imperishable Atman, the Universal Soul or God, there really was nothing left for the individual to strive for by way of attaining a moral or intellectual perfection, as man was essentially divine. Besides, indulging in vain speculations about the Universal Soul or God would divert his mind from ethical matters that were more important in the attainment of salvation. He stressed that it was only the practice of morality and meditation while treading the Path of Truth that could deliver an individual from evil. In the Buddha's philosophy, it was the moral kernel, his karma and not the immutable soul of the individual that endured the endless cycle of rebirth.

In his opinion, it was not outward appearance of modesty or piety that made one noble but the purity of one's thoughts, purged of all defilements and established in the eternal Dhamma that made one noble. He warned all those who employed unethical means in achieving their ends, either by resorting to violence or harming the innocent, that they would sooner or later, by virtue of their misdeeds, suffer the consequences of flouting the Dhamma.

The Buddha preached that it was only those who abided by the Dhamma, never veering from the Path of Truth who attained salvation. In fact, he did not regard a number of bhikkus who had not liberated their thoughts from the feeling of "I am" as enlightened beings, despite their rigorous spiritual training, and the realization that the self was in reality nothing more than a compound of mental and physical forces. The Buddha preached that it was this all-pervasive feeling of "I am" that gave birth to selfish desire, egotism and all the evils of worldly existence.

Therefore, he explained to his disciples that it was only upon the annihilation of the false idea of self and all selfish desires, that the mind purged of all impurities would be able to penetrate the Dhamma, thereby becoming an abode of the truth. According to the Buddha, there was indeed no rebirth for the individual who having habitually cultivated thoughts of selfless charity, universal love and compassion extended to the entire sentient creation, through the mindful and repeated destruction and prevention of the arising of all evil thoughts, had established himself in the eternal Dhamma.

THE EIGHTFOLD PATH

The entire philosophy of the Buddha, that deals primarily with the universal subject of human suffering, its origin and cessation, rests on the foundations of the Four Noble Truths that were revealed to him, at the time of "the awakening", in Bodhgaya, modern Bihar.

In the First Noble Truth, or the Truth of Suffering, the Buddha enunciated the immanent nature of suffering in human life. In his philosophy, it pervaded this entire world of change and experience. He preached that the birth of an individual marked the beginning of the inevitable suffering of disease, pain, decay, combination, separation, old age, lamentation and death. Suffering was the outcome of attachment to an imperfect, ever-changing, impermanent world and to all forms of worldly existence. The germ of suffering was in fact, present even in the five aggregates of attachment that composed the worldly self, namely, matter, feelings, perceptions, mind-objects and consciousness that were always in a state of flux. Thus, suffering, as defined by the Buddha, was "union with the unpleasant, the separation from the pleasant and the inability to achieve what one desires."

The Buddha preached in the Second Noble Truth or the Arising of Suffering, that it was thirst for sensual pleasure, existence and non-existence that caused the suffering of re-becoming and re-existence in this cycle of continuity, Samsara. It was this thirst conditioned by ignorance or the delusion that all worldly pleasures were everlasting which caused the individual to seek the intransient in a transient world of name and form, thereby subjecting him to the pain and suffering of continual rebirth.

The Buddha impressed upon his followers that the false idea of the eternity of the self or soul, believed to be a part of the all- pervasive Universal Soul, the Atman or God, perpetuated the thirst for existence. This thirst survived the death of the individual, manifesting itself in a new form of life, in this cycle of continuity. Indeed, it was ignorance that even created the thirst for the non-existence of all unpleasant experiences, causing pain and suffering to the individual, as he struggled in vain, to achieve a perfect state of existence in this imperfect, ever-changing world of ours.

However, the Buddha certified in the Third Noble Truth or the Cessation of Suffering that there is a remedy to suffering, which is the Fourth Noble Truth or the Eightfold Path of Righteousness. This path leads to the cessation of suffering, enlightenment and a permanent release from the painful cycle of rebirth. The Noble Eightfold Path was neither one of extreme self-indulgence nor of extreme asceticism, both of which the Buddha found unworthy and unprofitable in the realization of the ultimate truth. It was, in fact, the middle path that advocated moderation, as the Buddha believed that both the body and mind needed nourishment whilst performing advanced forms of meditation.

The path aimed at achieving a moral and intellectual perfection. This perfection, the Buddha believed, cleansed the mind of all impurities, thereby making it conducive to the realization of the ultimate reality. Moreover, the Eightfold Path that was governed by the principles of universal love and compassion extended to the entire sentient creation, enjoined the cultivation of certain noble qualities of the heart, such as selfless charity, tolerance and above all the sentiment of loving-kindness, in one's dealings with the wider world.

In the Buddha's philosophy, the term compassion was not just limited to sympathy, as commonly understood by most people, but extended to feelings of sympathetic joy, that meant rejoicing in the fortunes of others, and also, as mentioned above, loving-kindness which meant treating humankind, despite their failings, with unfailing kindness and love. The Buddha believed that by ethical behaviour and the development of the intellect through the practice of introspective meditation, whilst treading the Path of Righteousness, the individual could ultimately gain an insight into the truth of things and thus be freed from the endless cycle of rebirth.

The Eightfold Path as laid out by the Buddha comprised – Right Understanding, Right Thought, Right Speech, Right Action, Right Livelihood, Right Effort, Right Mindfulness and Right Concentration, the belief and practice of which according to the Buddha led to enlightenment and emancipation from this cycle of continuity, Samsara.

The Buddha laid stress on the importance of the Right Understanding of the Four Noble Truths, in the removal of all errors of judgement that enabled an individual to gauge situations correctly. According to the Buddha, it was the wisdom attained by a deep and thorough understanding of the Four Noble Truths, that gave the individual a penetrating insight into the Dhamma, and made him see things as they are. He further stressed on the cultivation of Right Thoughts that were governed by the principles of selfless charity, boundless love and compassion extended to humankind, irrespective of religion, class or creed.

By the practice of Right Speech, the Buddha entreated his followers to abstain from lying, slander, abuse, gossip and all the evils of the tongue that would cause others to react in undesirable ways, thereby creating disharmony in society. He also impressed upon his followers the importance of Right Action, enjoining them to abstain from murder, theft, adultery and such acts that would sow seeds of dissension in society, gradually eating into its moral fibre.

Through the Right Means of Livelihood, the Buddha aimed above all else, at promoting peace and harmony in the world. He preached the earning of one's livelihood through honourable means, without trading in arms and ammunition, illicit liquor or indulging in any activity that would breed hatred and enmity, leading to violence and anarchy in society. It must be borne in mind that Buddhism is essentially a religion of universal love and peace, and even the mere suggestion of bloodshed and war, no matter how great or justified the cause, goes against the teachings of Lord Buddha.

Right Effort as preached by the Buddha, implies the energetic will to cultivate wholesome states of mind by the complete expunging of selfish desires and all the impurities in it. It enjoins the cultivation of only good and pure thoughts that are rooted in truth, which the Buddha believed created a tranquil state of mind that was essential in the realization of the ultimate reality. The Buddha urged his followers, to consciously prevent the arising of evil thoughts and to bring to perfection all good thoughts present in their minds.

He further preached that by exercising the Right kind of Mindfulness, by constantly being conscious and objective about the nature of his immediate physical and mental states, the individual could succeed in dispelling all negative feelings of anxiety, doubt, anger and worry that were impeding his progress on the path to salvation. He would thereby cultivate a more positive frame of mind, which would help him discern the good from the evil as he strove along.

By Right Concentration, the Buddha meant that the individual through the practice of meditation or the four dhyanas, would acquire a one-pointedness of concentration which was important in the realization of the truth. Meditation, in the Buddha's philosophy, was essential in disciplining the mind, as it gradually purged it of all impurities.

Indeed, as experienced in the first stage of meditation or dhyana, all negative thoughts or impurities such as sensuousness, anger and worry are dispelled and feelings of joy and happiness retained. At this stage the mind is still active though in the second stage of dhyana all mental activities are suspended. In this stage of meditation, feelings of joy and happiness remain and a one-pointedness of concentration is developed. As one progresses to the third stage, feelings of joy disappear though happiness is still there and the mind is peaceful. In the fourth stage of dhyana there are no sensations whatsoever, as the mind transcends all feelings of happiness and unhappiness, and is in a state of pure equanimity – a state that is very conducive to attaining the supreme wisdom. The practice of these four dhyanas form the basis for deep insight meditation, as practised by the Buddha.

Thus, in the Buddha's prescription for salvation, all the divisions of the Eightfold Path were to be followed simultaneously by the meditator, in the achievement of the moral and intellectual ideal that would give him a penetrating insight into the reality of this universe, upon the attainment of enlightenment. It was only through the belief and practice of the sacred truths and above all, by treading the Noble Eightfold Path of Righteousness or the Fourth Noble Truth, as preached by the Buddha, that an individual enjoyed the unconditioned bliss and freedom of Nirvana that emancipated him from this cycle of continuity, Samsara.

VARIED VERSES

These varied verses reflect the Buddha's concern about the salvation of mankind, attained through the belief and practice of the Four Noble Truths.

Above all, they highlight the pragmatism of the Buddha's doctrine that advocated the importance of treading the Noble Eightfold Path or the middle path in the attainment of the eternal bliss of Nirvana. It must be borne in mind that the Noble Eightfold Path was suited not only to the monks who had chosen the renunciant way of life but also to the laity who could continue to live in this world and perform their household duties. The Buddha was a pragmatist who believed in the performance of one's duty towards one's family as well as society. This was one of the major conditions conducive to the happiness of the individual. He regarded asceticism and retirement into the forest without fulfilling one's obligations towards one's family as escapism, a condition that did not contribute to the general well being of the individual or society.

Therefore, the Buddha advised his followers to seek, above all, happiness and fulfillment in their work, in the performance of their duties, as he impressed upon them the importance of economic prosperity in promoting peace and harmony in the world. He preached that immorality, violence and crime were the outcome of poverty and economic hardship and were signs of an angry society.

However, the Buddha's teachings were not just directed to the material well being in the attainment of happiness but also to the moral and intellectual development of an individual that would lead to a happier state of existence. He believed that if each individual strove for the ultimate truth, whilst treading the Eightfold Path of Righteousness, then collectively as members of a community they could create conditions that would promote an atmosphere of peace, goodwill and understanding all over the world.

The Buddha did not deny the feeling of happiness attained through the individual's satisfying experiences with the external world. He preached that though the lesser happiness in the worldly sense did contribute to an individual's general well being, a condition that was conducive to higher spiritual and intellectual attainments, it paled significantly in comparison to the abiding happiness of Nirvana, born out of strenuous effort by steadfastly treading the Path of Truth. He believed that those who were truly wise would go in search of the eternal bliss of Nirvana instead of seeking the lesser, impermanent worldly happiness.

Indeed, the Buddha was convinced about the efficacy of the Eightfold Path that enabled those who followed it, to see the light of wisdom through the practice of morality and mindful meditation, which in turn helped them to discern the good from the evil, as they worked their way towards salvation.

He also stressed that as long as one remained in bondage to selfish desires, one would continue to suffer the pain of repeated existence in this cycle of continuity, Samsara. In the Buddha's philosophy, it was only through the practice of mental discipline and the complete expunging of all selfish desires, that the mind purged of all impurities would be able to realize the ultimate truth.

Buddhism is optimistic, in the sense, that it holds the hope of salvation for even the evil-doer. By simply entering and steadfastly treading the Noble Eightfold Path of Righteousness, he can negate his misdeeds or bad karma. The Buddha believed that the evil-doer through moral conduct and mental discipline acquired through the practice of mindful meditation, could also gradually attain the supreme wisdom whilst treading the upward Path of Righteousness. By mindfully meditating upon his immediate mental states, he could trace the source of his negative thoughts and feelings, and thereby purge his mind of all impurities.

In the Buddha's philosophy, it was "volition", the intention or choice that was of ultimate significance in determining one's destiny in this world and beyond. Having chosen, an individual acted through his thoughts, words, and deeds, the consequences of which he had to bear through innumerable births in this cycle of continuity. It must be borne in mind that the Buddha regarded "choice" or "volition" as one's karma, as it was the mental action that preceded all thoughts and deeds.

Thus, the Buddha viewed mental volition that he equated with will or the thirst for existence, as one's karma. This thirst that survived the death of the individual was a powerful force that caused whole lives, in fact the whole world to move forward in good, bad or neutral directions.

The will or the thirst for existence was conditioned by the false idea of the immortality of the self or the human soul that arose from ignorance about the nature of reality. It was in fact, ignorance or delusion that led the individual to believe that the world held some everlasting pleasures and satisfactions, causing him to seek satiety and permanence in an imperfect, ever-changing world. In fact, according to the Buddha, it was this false idea of self that created selfishness and all the evils of worldly existence.

He preached that the idea of the eternal soul or self was merely an illusion and that the only thing that survived the endless cycle of rebirths was one's karma or deeds that shaped one's character in this life and after. He impressed upon his followers the importance of the Law of Karma, of cause and effect that governed the course of their lives, in this cycle of continuity. According to the Law of Karma, good deeds endowed a person with physical well being, fortune and happiness whilst bad deeds subjected him to a life of misery, sorrow and hardship. Thus, an individual reaped what he had sown in his present as well as in all his past lives. It was simply by virtue of his good or bad karma that he was born in happy or unhappy circumstances. There was in reality no God or any supernatural power sitting on moral judgement, who meted out rewards or punishments for his deeds in this world and beyond.

Therefore, the Buddha warned all those guilty of adultery, theft and other evils of earthly existence who had entered the downward path of falsehood, that although their actions brought them momentary pleasure, they would sooner or later bear the bitter fruits of their unrighteous behaviour. The Law of Karma would eventually prevail, and the evil-doers would suffer the consequences of their misdeeds, as they lived in a hell of their own creation, in this world itself. Their minds would be tormented by feelings of guilt and remorse, while they prayed in vain for a restful sleep and a peaceful state of mind.

The Buddha further preached that it was only upon the extinction of the illusion of self, the thirst for existence and all worldly attachments that the individual would be able to attain the eternal bliss of Nirvana. He explained that through moral conduct and mindful meditation whilst treading the Path of Righteousness, an individual could attain the supreme wisdom and liberate himself from the cycle of rebirth. The choice of treading the upward Path of Truth or the downward path of evil and pleasure lay entirely with him – the former leading to deliverance and the latter to sorrow and suffering.

THE ELEPHANT

In Indian folklore, the elephant has always been revered as a symbol of unmatched wisdom, strength and forbearance who despite having endured every kind of hardship on the battlefield, remained fiercely loyal to his master, regardless of victory or defeat. In fact, Indra the Lord of the Gods of the Vedic pantheon used the elephant as his mount and the Buddha himself in Buddhist literature was likened to an elephant, patiently bearing every form of hardship, as he strove tirelessly through innumerable births, towards salvation.

According to the Buddha, a tamed elephant used by kings and warriors on the battlefield quietly bore the pain inflicted by the arrows shot at him, carrying his master to victory. With the same nobility of soul, an enlightened being attained salvation, after patiently enduring the pain and suffering of human life, without ever veering from the Path of Righteousness.

However, the Buddha preached that victory brought to the warrior on the battlefield by his elephant paled in comparison to the conquest of the self through individual effort whilst treading the Eightfold Path to salvation. He believed that the individual who through ethical behaviour and the practice of insight meditation had attained enlightenment and liberated himself from the cycle of rebirth was wise like the elephant who carried his master to victory. He realized the impermanence of hard times as he steadfastly walked the Noble Path, ever-hopeful that they would soon be followed by happier ones. However, the Buddha laid stress not on external aid but on human endeavour in the attainment of salvation.

He further preached that the root cause of suffering was ignorance that created the thirst for separate existence and attachment to all things worldly, subjecting the individual to repeated existence in this imperfect, impermanent world. According to the Buddha, it was only upon the utter extinction of all forms of thirst and worldly attachments through the removal of ignorance, by treading the Path of Righteousness that an individual could gain an insight into reality and thus be freed from the painful cycle of rebirth. The enlightened being would then realize the transient nature of all forms of sensual pleasures and worldly existence as he dwelt in the eternal bliss of Nirvana.

Moreover, the awakened one would also realize that in reality there is no "self" or an eternal, unchanging soul, the mover behind all movements, but one's karma or deeds of the present and past lives that endures the cycle of rebirths. That what we perceive as a "self" or the "I" is in truth, only a compound of five mental and physical aggregates, a product of a series of causes and effects that can be traced to the dawn of the evolution of one's consciousness. It is the Law of Karma or the law of cause and effect that governs the affairs of men. According to this law, an individual suffers pain or experiences happiness by virtue of his own deeds and misdeeds in this cycle of rebirth. Thus, the present reaps what the past has sown.

However, upon the extinction of the illusion of the self, by treading the Path of Righteousness, the individual would succeed in overcoming the thirst for existence and all worldly attachments, as he entered the indescribable realm of the ultimate truth, Nirvana. By training his mind through the practice of self-restraint and meditation, as he steered clear of the path of evil and temptation in the attainment of salvation, he would be like an elephant who had extricated himself from the mud and continued his journey on the cleaner path towards his ultimate destination – victory.

THIRST

According to the words of Siddhartha Gautama the Buddha preserved in the ancient Buddhist scriptures -"It is thirst which produces re-existence and re-becoming, and which is bound up with passionate greed, and which finds fresh delight now here, now there, namely 1. thirst for sensual pleasures, 2. thirst for existence and becoming and 3. thirst for non-existence." Although thirst is the most palpable cause of suffering, it must be remembered that it arises out of ignorance of the Four Noble Truths and belief in the false idea of self.

The Buddha preached that it is the right understanding of the Four Noble Truths through moral conduct and practice of insight meditation, whilst treading the Eightfold Path of Righteousness, that gives an individual a penetrating insight into the Dhamma upon the extinction of thirst. The enlightened individual then has the right perception of reality that all worldly things and forms of existence are a product of a series of causes and effects that can be traced back to beginningless time. There is in reality no perfect state of existence nor anything permanent in the world that can bring abiding joy to him. It is indeed ignorance that creates thirst for sensual pleasure and existence, causing the individual to seek satiety and permanence in an imperfect, ever-changing world of time and succession.

In his philosophy, it was ignorance that created the false idea of "self" or the "soul", the "I" or ego, as an immutable, unchanging, permanent entity that survived the death of an individual. It was belief in the eternity of the human soul or self as a part of the all-pervasive Universal Soul or Self, that gave birth to selfhood and other evils. The Buddha thus traced the cause for the insatiable thirst for sensual pleasures, existence as a separate creature as well as the non-existence of unpleasant and painful experiences and situations to ignorance, which subjected the individual to continual existence in the cycle of rebirth.

For he believed that the thirst for sensual pleasures whether carnal, olfactory or tactile, drove the individual to seek satisfaction, quite often at the expense of the happiness of others, thereby negating the good karma of his present as well as of his past births.

The Buddha impressed upon his followers that the illusion of self also gave rise to the thirst for separate existence and becoming in this world and beyond. It was human nature to desire to become other than what one is, and it was this desire or thirst that caused becoming and re-existence in this world of change and experience. According to him, there was no "being" as such in this empirical universe and that all individuals were always in a state of becoming, with each state of existence causing and conditioning the next.

Indeed, the Buddha who equated thirst with "mental volition", or will for existence, regarded it as the most powerful force in the world. It had its roots in ignorance about the reality of the universe, and caused lives and the whole world in fact, to move forward in good, bad or neutral directions. He believed that it was only when the volition, will or the selfish desire for existence was utterly extinguished in the mind, that an individual could attain the sublime bliss of Nirvana.

The Buddha further explained to his followers, that the thirst for non-existence of unpleasant or painful experiences, which he regarded as revulsion for reality, caused an individual to resort to escapism and unrighteous forms of behaviour in overcoming all the hardships of worldly existence. He preached that those who failed to cope with the trials and tribulations of life and resorted to drugs, alcohol or in extreme cases suicide, instead of negating their bad karma by entering the Path of Truth, were subjecting themselves to more suffering. It was only those who endured their suffering patiently as they strove earnestly along the Path of Truth, who were assured of salvation.

Thus, it was upon the removal of the veil of ignorance through moral conduct and the practice of insight meditation, when the thirst for sensual pleasure, existence and non-existence would be expunged, that an individual could attain the unconditioned bliss of Nirvana.

THE BHIKKU

The word "bhikku" literally means a mendicant, one who lives on the alms given by others. In ancient India, the ascetics who had renounced the world in search of the ultimate truth were referred to as bhikkus and it was customary for bhikkus to stand with their begging bowls at the doorstep of householders, graciously accepting whatever was given to them. They asked and craved for nothing and it was considered the moral duty of the householders not to send them away empty handed.

In fact, the Sangha or the order of monks that the Buddha founded shortly after his enlightenment comprised the five bhikkus in whose company he had practised his severe austerities in the jungles of Uruvela. Referring to the first converts to his faith as bhikkus, he enjoined them to help each other out as they trod the Path of Righteousness, spreading the truth in all the four corners of the world. Thus, all the monks of the Buddhist faith were called bhikkus and later upon the ordination of Mahapajapati Gautami, all the women who were admitted into the Sangha were referred to as bhikkunis.

The Buddha in his sermons to the bhikkus impressed upon them the importance of following the middle path that lay between extreme asceticism and self-indulgence in the attainment of salvation, as he believed that the mind and body needed nourishment while practising advanced forms of meditation. He therefore dismissed the practice of extreme asceticism followed by some of the most renowned sages of his time, whereby they inflicted the severest forms of physical tortures upon themselves in an attempt to purify their souls in the attainment of salvation, as unworthy and unprofitable. He even dismissed the path of self-indulgence followed by those who sought happiness through the fulfillment of sensual desires as unworthy and unprofitable.

In the Buddha's philosophy it was only the middle path or the Noble Eightfold Path, based on the values of universal love and compassion, that led to the extinction of all selfish desires and the realization of the ultimate reality. The Buddha further preached that it was through the practice of morality and self-discipline of the mind, body and senses whilst treading the Path of Truth, that an individual could attain enlightenment and thus be released from the endless cycle of rebirth.

According to him, those ordained as monks or bhikkus, though on the path of enlightenment, were not assured of salvation unless they purged their minds of all selfish desires and worldly attachments. More importantly, he preached, that it was upon the extinction of the illusion of the "self", of the expunging of the feeling of "I am", that a bhikku could attain salvation.

The Buddha further warned the bhikkus of the evils of star gazing, magic and astrology, urging them to work out their own salvation with diligence. He also advised them against using their spiritual knowledge in manipulating the minds of the people in order to amass wealth and said that any bhikku guilty of such an offence would cease to be a bhikku.

Above all, he entreated the bhikkus to master the Dhamma, the eternal law, as they steadfastly walked along the Path of Truth, and to spread it across the seven seas, so that the entire universe would be illumined by the infinite light of truth.

Indeed, in the Buddha's philosophy a true bhikku was one whose mind purged of all evil had become the abode of the truth. By spreading the Buddha's message of loving-kindness that transcended all barriers of religion, class or creed and by treating humankind with unfailing love and compassion, he brought hope and peace to a world shrouded in the darkness of despair.

THE BRAHMIN

The Buddha esteemed a true Brahmin highly, regarding him as the embodiment of wisdom and virtue. The Brahmins, the exalted class of priests in India, were the law makers who interpreted the Dhamma, the moral law, for the people. In the Buddha's philosophy, it was not through birth, lineage or wealth that an individual could claim the high status of a Brahmin but through the nobility of his thoughts, words and deeds.

Anyone, irrespective of his religion, class or creed, through moral conduct and the attainment of wisdom could climb the social ladder and become a Brahmin. Indeed, the Buddha recognized only those individuals who having extinguished all selfish desires for sensual pleasures, existence and non-existence had realized the ultimate reality, as true Brahmins.

In ancient India and even later, the Brahmins or priests along with the Kshatriyas or warriors and kings ruled over the Vaishyas, the commoners who were husbandmen and the rest of the populace. However, the Brahmins were not necessarily hereditary priests, they were also intellectuals, landowners and a number of them were also engaged in trade.

Although the Buddha respected a true Brahmin for his wisdom and learning, he had scant respect for those Brahmins who made a living through sorcery or for those who misused their spiritual knowledge by manipulating the minds of the people. The Buddha who had been a student of the Brahmins, neither recognized those who enjoined the performance of meaningless rituals in an attempt to extort money from the people nor those who practised extreme forms of asceticism, with hatred and desire in their hearts, subjecting themselves to every form of hardship in order to attain salvation, as true Brahmins.

However, the Buddha acknowledged the contribution of Brahmins to society, for they were the law makers who laid down the rules of the caste system that has right through the ages preserved the integrity of Indian society, despite the social upheavals that followed innumerable foreign invasions in India. The laws for all the castes, enjoined the performance of one's duty to one's family and community, in accordance with the Dhamma, and salvation was the ultimate goal for all.

However, with a large number of Brahmins arrogating more powers to themselves by guarding their spiritual knowledge jealously in order to retain their control over the religious lives of the people, the Buddha challenged their supremacy by simply showing the Noble Eightfold Path to salvation, thereby demonstrating to the world that spiritual attainment was not the preserve of the Brahmins and the upper classes. He preached that it was not purity of birth, wealth or position that determined the exalted rank of a Brahmin but the possession of the qualities of wisdom and virtue. Anyone could by treading the Eightfold Path of Righteousness and by extinguishing all selfish desires, acquire wisdom and thus be released from the painful cycle of rebirth. Indeed, there was no karmic residue for the true Brahmin who by leading a life of virtue and righteousness, in accordance with the Dhamma had realized the ultimate reality, Nirvana.

BIBLIOGRAPHY

Basham, A.L. *The Wonder that was India*. New Delhi: Rupa and Company, 1954, 2003.

Byrom, Thomas. *The Dhammapada – The Sayings of the Buddha*. London: Random House, 1976, 2002.

Carrithers, Michael. *The Buddha*. New York: Oxford University Press, 1983, 1996.

Carus, Paul. *The Gospel of Buddha*. Oxford: One Word Publications, 1994.

Davids, T W Rhys. *Buddhist India*. Delhi: Motilal Banarsidass,1903, 1997.

———. *Early Buddhism*. New Delhi: Asian Educational Services,1908, 2002.

Easwaran, Eknath. *The Dhammapada*. New Delhi: Penguin Books India (P) Ltd, 1986, 1996.

Radhakrishnan, S. *The Dhammapada*. New Delhi: Oxford University Press, 1950, 1999.

Rahula, Sri Walpola. *What The Buddha Taught*. Sri Lanka: Buddhist Cultural Centre, 1996.

Saint-Hilaire, J Barthelemy. *Buddhism – Life, Teachings and Religion of Buddha*. Delhi: Adarsh Enterprises, 2002.